History for All the People:

*One Hundred Years of Public History
in North Carolina*

NORTH CAROLINA DEPARTMENT OF CULTURAL RESOURCES

LISBETH C. EVANS
Secretary

OFFICE OF ARCHIVES AND HISTORY

JEFFREY J. CROW
Deputy Secretary

DIVISION OF HISTORICAL RESOURCES

DAVID J. OLSON
Director

HISTORICAL PUBLICATIONS SECTION

DONNA E. KELLY
Administrator

Printed by Edwards Brothers Incorporated

History for All the People:

One Hundred Years of Public History in North Carolina

Ansley Herring Wegner

Office of Archives and History
North Carolina Department of Cultural Resources
Raleigh

Foreword

A centennial is an important milestone in the history of any institution. As the deputy secretary of the Office of Archives and History, I wear several hats, including those of state historic preservation officer, coordinator of the State Historical Records Advisory Board, and secretary of the North Carolina Historical Commission. At the seventy-fifth anniversary of the North Carolina Historical Commission in 1978, I doubt that I even considered being present for the centennial of the commission. Now it is my honor to preside over the venerable state agency in its one-hundredth year.

When I joined the staff of Archives and History as heritage consultant for the American Revolution Bicentennial Committee in 1974 fresh out of graduate school at Duke University, the agency was one-half its present size in number of employees. Its expenditures, moreover, were one-eighth the present amount. Despite recent budgetary crises that have affected all of state government, the North Carolina Office of Archives and History remains one of the largest and most comprehensive state public history agencies in the nation.

The one-hundred-year legacy of Archives and History underscores two abiding features about the preservation of North Carolina's heritage. First, the people of North Carolina treasure their history. The General Assembly has provided the necessary funding to allow the programs of Archives and History to grow and to make available a wide range of services. Second, the people of North Carolina have been well served by a professional and dedicated staff whose work is highly regarded and respected.

At the seventy-fifth anniversary of the North Carolina Literary and Historical Association in 1975, Frontis W. Johnston, the Davidson College historian, remarked: "Every organization as old as ours has some history to lean on, some history to overcome, and some history to make." As Archives and History enters its second century, it continues a long tradition of excellence in the service of history. Yet, as William S. Price Jr., former director of Archives and History, once observed: "We forget the 'public' in public history only at our peril." That sense of public service impels the staff of Archives and History. That dedication has led hundreds of employees—upwards of 2,800 over the course of 100 years—to devote all or part of their careers to furthering the promotion and preservation of this state's history.

In writing this new history of the agency, Ansley Herring Wegner has placed the service commitment at the center of her story. Receiving less attention are the inevitable organizational and personnel changes. Highlighted separately in accompanying features are initiatives and programs, some ongoing, some long since concluded. Assisting Ansley in preparing the twenty sidebars devoted to specific topics were her colleagues in the Research Branch, Michael Hill, Dennis F. Daniels, and Mark Anderson Moore.

History for All the People, the title of the book and the theme of the centennial commemoration, was a slogan applied to Archives and History programming by Christopher Crittenden, director from 1935 to 1968. "Our histories should be something of broad, general interest—not merely for the professional historians, not merely for the genealogists, not just for any other limited group, but instead for the people at large," Crittenden wrote in 1941. "There are opportunities in this realm of which we have only begun to take advantage," he declared. Crittenden's words are as timely today as they were more than a half century ago.

Jeffrey J. Crow, *Deputy Secretary*
Office of Archives and History

Table of Contents

A view of Warsaw, North Carolina, in the 1920s. This Duplin County town hails as the site of the North Carolina Historical Commission's first meeting on November 20, 1903. Photograph reproduced courtesy of the Duplin County Tourism office.

1

The "Aughts": A Chance Beginning, A Solid Start

It was a surreptitious meeting that marked the first gathering of the North Carolina Historical Commission, the predecessor of the present-day Office of Archives and History. The five original members of the commission were selected geographically to ensure that all regions of the state were represented. That geographic diversity made meeting arrangements difficult, especially when there were no reimbursements available for expenses. After several unsuccessful attempts to gather a quorum of three, Raleigh attorney William J. Peele—the initiator of the March 7, 1903, resolution that became Chapter 767 of the Public Laws, establishing the Historical Commission—devised a way to muster a meeting. Upon learning that fellow commission member James D. Hufham, a Baptist minister from Henderson, was visiting his daughter in Duplin County during the fall of 1903, Peele resolved to join another member of the body and pay a surprise call on Hufham. Peele persuaded R. D. W. Connor, a high school principal from Wilmington, to board a train and meet him in the small Duplin County town of Warsaw, where they found Hufham and launched the North Carolina Historical Commission at a meeting of the three held November 20, 1903.

At the meeting Peele was elected chairman and Connor secretary. The commission granted fifty dollars to Fred A. Olds, collector for the Hall of History, predecessor to the Museum of History, for use in making photographic reproductions for that collection. The trio then established three prizes for writing. Winners would receive one hundred dollars for the best essays in each of the following categories: biographical sketches of North Carolinians, county histories, and essays covering a decade in North Carolina history. There is no record of the writing contests beyond those preliminary discussions. Connor recalled, years later, that the competitions evinced little interest. The group also allocated ten dollars for an advertisement in the *North Carolina Booklet* that described the Historical Commission's work.

The November 1903 gathering was the only meeting of the initial board—which consisted of Peele, Connor, Hufham, Forster A. Sondley of Asheville, and

Richard Dixon Dillard of Edenton—during its first two-year term. There was no office or staff, and the operating budget was five hundred dollars per year. The Historical Commission's first publication, *Literary and Historical Activities in North Carolina, 1900-1905*, a compendium by Peele and Clarence Poe, was published in 1907; it had been an endeavor discussed at the outset. Similarly, the commission prepared and published the first biennial report, covering 1903 to 1905.

R. D. W. Connor (1878-1950), a founding member of the North Carolina Historical Commission, led and served the organization in various capacities until his death.

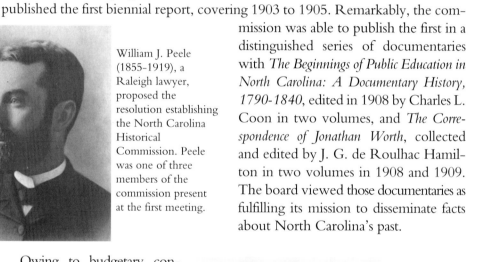

William J. Peele (1855-1919), a Raleigh lawyer, proposed the resolution establishing the North Carolina Historical Commission. Peele was one of three members of the commission present at the first meeting.

Remarkably, the commission was able to publish the first in a distinguished series of documentaries with *The Beginnings of Public Education in North Carolina: A Documentary History, 1790-1840*, edited in 1908 by Charles L. Coon in two volumes, and *The Correspondence of Jonathan Worth*, collected and edited by J. G. de Roulhac Hamilton in two volumes in 1908 and 1909. The board viewed those documentaries as fulfilling its mission to disseminate facts about North Carolina's past.

Owing to budgetary constraints and the inability to assemble its members, the Historical Commission languished until the legislature in 1907 amended the original act. The new act broadened the powers of the commission, increased the budget to five thousand dollars (with members also being permitted reimbursement for expenses encountered in attending meetings), and allowed for the employment of a

James D. Hufham (1834-1921), a Baptist minister and editor, was present at the first meeting of the North Carolina Historical Commission.

R. D. W. Connor:
Setting the Professional Standard

Robert Digges Wimberly Connor, the fourth of twelve children, was born in Wilson on September 26, 1878, to Henry Groves and Kate Whitfield Connor. He completed his public education in the Wilson County schools and went on to the University of North Carolina (UNC), from which he graduated in 1899. Ambitious and industrious even then, Connor during his senior year at UNC served as editor of all three of the university's student publications—the newspaper, the yearbook, and the literary magazine. Following graduation Connor taught in the public schools in Winston and Wilmington and served in school administration in Wilmington and Oxford. It was during his employment in Winston that he met and married Sadie Hanes of

R. D. W. Connor (*far left, center*) is seen here with his family on the porch of his parents' Wilson home around 1900. Henry Groves Connor and his wife Kate are in the top right of the frame. The elder Connor served as a North Carolina Supreme Court justice and judge in the U.S. Court for the Eastern District of North Carolina.

Mocksville, a teacher. While in Wilmington in 1903, Connor accepted an appointment to the newly formed North Carolina Historical Commission. He worked for four years as the unpaid secretary of the commission while gainfully employed in the public schools or with the Department of Public Instruction, promoting public education through speeches and articles, proving his ability to perform varied and complex jobs simultaneously.

In 1906 Connor accepted a salaried position with the Historical Commission, and his stalwart leadership and investigative mind guided the agency through its early years. In particular he recognized the importance of a state archival program. With the Historical Commission firmly established in 1920, Connor pursued graduate studies at Columbia University in preparation for returning to his alma mater to teach. In 1921 he tendered his resignation to accept the Kenan Professorship in History and Government at UNC. While in that post, his contributions to the archival profession were brought to the attention of President Franklin D. Roosevelt. With confirmation of both Connor's Democratic loyalties and professional reputation, Roosevelt appointed Connor as the first Archivist of the United States in 1934. Once again Connor found himself having to build an archival program from the ground up. He successfully educated the Washington bureaucrats about the need for proper records management and justified the urgency for protecting records of archival quality. He remained Archivist of the United States until 1941, when he gave in to his first love and returned to teach history in Chapel Hill.

Connor's devotion to the North Carolina Historical Commission and later the Executive Board of what was then the Department of Archives and History continued as he held tenure as a member and later chairman until his death in 1950. Similarly, he served his beloved UNC as secretary to its Board of Trustees, president of its General Alumni Association, and head of its Department of History and Government. In the midst of World War II, in an address he delivered after being sworn in as president of the Society of American Archivists, R. D. W. Connor defined the role of archivists and all public historians when he said: "We are the custodians of the accumulated evidences of those traditions and ideals of democracy and freedom for which we fight and without which . . . no such peace can be established or maintained in the world."—*Ansley Herring Wegner*

The North Carolina Literary and Historical Association: The Fountainhead

On October 23, 1900, in the Olivia Raney Library, located at that time near the State Capitol, a group of men and women convened the organizational meeting of the State Literary and Historical Association. Just as candidate for governor Charles B. Aycock sought to redeem the state from a legacy of ignorance, the members of the association sought to raise the cultural sights of citizens. Early leaders made it their task to "correct printed misrepresentations about the state." J. Bryan Grimes, who took office as secretary of state when Aycock acceded to the governorship the following year, persuaded the group to address perceived slights. Members issued a detailed position in support of a famed boast concerning services rendered by North Carolina soldiers during the Civil War: "First at Bethel, Farthest at Gettysburg and Chickamauga, and Last at Appomattox." A publication by that title appeared in 1907 under the auspices of the North Carolina Historical Commission. It was the commission's first imprint.

Walter Clark (1846-1924), a Civil War veteran, chief justice of the North Carolina Supreme Court, and compiler of *The State Records of North Carolina*, was the first president of the North Carolina Literary and Historical Association, 1900-1901.

In January 1903 the association passed a resolution calling for the creation of the Historical Commission. A legislative bill to that effect, drafted by Raleigh lawyer William J. Peele, was enacted into law two months later. Since that time, the histories of the association and the commission have been intertwined. "Lit and Hist" has played a key role in the cultural life of the state. The group has failed to meet only once—during the 1918 influenza epidemic. Its most conspicuous activity has been the annual meeting. Keynote speakers over the years have included former presidents William Howard Taft and Harry S. Truman; writers Thomas Wolfe, Inglis Fletcher, and Charles Frazier; and scholars U. B. Phillips, Guion Johnson, and Blyden Jackson. Offspring of the association have included many state cultural groups, among them the North

full-time secretary. The first secretary, whose term of service commenced July 1, 1907, was R. D. W. Connor, who set up offices in the northeast corner of the State Capitol at the end of the east gallery of the Senate chamber. There the commission could collect, arrange systematically, and protect from damage records of historical significance that previously had been, as Connor reported, "stuffed away in dark pigeonholes, in boxes and corners, without order or system . . . tossed about from place to place with an utter indifference to their value, or . . . thrown helter-skelter here and there, in leaky attics in various parts of the city." To assist Connor in his duties, two more staffers were brought on board—William Weaver in 1907 as a janitor and Mrs. W. S. Wilson in 1908 as a stenographer.

The Historical Commission's most important perceived obligation to the state was to collect, edit, and publish historical documents. The desire was to make the records, both public and private, available to the citizens and to ensure their

Carolina Folklore Society (formed in 1913), the North Carolina Art Society (1923), the North Carolina Society for the Preservation of Antiquities [now Preservation North Carolina] (1939), and the North Carolina Archaeological Society (1939). In order that all groups might coordinate the respective annual convocations, "Lit and Hist" for many years sponsored "Culture Week," a week-long series of meetings, generally in Raleigh. In time, however, interest and membership in the parent organization lagged.

In a 1967 memorandum entitled "Whither Now?," Christopher Crittenden, the longtime director of Archives and History, suggested that the future of the association, then 2,100 members strong, needed study. "Originally this was a kind of pump-priming operation, but now not only is the pump running at full capacity but a veritable flood is flowing forth," Crittenden observed. He suggested that the association either be recast as the North Carolina Historical Association, forsaking the traditional literary role, or that Culture Week be scaled back. The latter recommendation was adopted, and the annual meeting was reduced to a single day. At present the group numbers approximately 330 members, who receive the *North Carolina Historical Review* and *Carolina Comments* and since 1992 have had the opportunity to subscribe to the *North Carolina Literary Review.* "Lit and Hist" administers book award competitions in fiction, poetry, nonfiction, and juvenile literature. Separate contests are held to judge the year's best literary magazines at the middle and high school levels and the best scholarly papers on state history. The Christopher Crittenden Memorial Award recognizes significant contributions to the preservation of North Carolina history, while the R. Hunt Parker Memorial Award acknowledges similar literary contributions.—*Michael Hill*

The literary awards presented by the North Carolina Literary and Historical Association are housed in a display case on the third floor of the Archives and History/State Library Building. Award competitions are administered annually for works of nonfiction, fiction, poetry, and juvenile literature by North Carolina authors.

preservation. During that time the Historical Commission was able to accomplish its goal—first, by bringing records into physical and intellectual control as the State Archives and, second, by publishing documentary volumes. Of research value to this day, the books from the Historical Commission's first decade include *The Papers of Archibald D. Murphey,* edited by William Henry Hoyt; *The Papers of Thomas Ruffin,* collected and edited by J. G. de Roulhac Hamilton; and *North Carolina Schools and Academies, 1790-1840,* edited by Charles L. Coon.

In a further effort to help educate the public, Connor prepared the materials for "North Carolina Day" in the public schools. North Carolina Day, authorized by the legislature in 1901, was celebrated in the public schools until 1914. Each year the schools hosted the event to celebrate some aspect of the state's history, with the hope that the exercises would instill interest and pride in the state's heritage. Connor compiled essays for publication and study on the subjects

The Pleasant Retreat Academy in Lincolnton. In 1908 the North Carolina legislature appropriated funds to the Lincolnton UDC to purchase the building and use it as a museum.

selected for many of the annual programs. Implicit in that effort was a desire to provide educational materials directly to public schoolteachers in order to supplement North Carolina history textbooks. In 1907 Connor expressed his conviction that "surely it would be difficult to find a more important or a more inspiring work than to teach the children of North Carolina to know their State and to develop in them a desire to serve the State, based upon knowledge of the Past and Present, and an intelligent forecast of her future." To that end, the Historical Commission issued leaflets and reprints of historical documents. In an attempt to glean information about North Carolina as a colony and a nascent state—an era during which newspapers were not published there on a regular basis—the commission also authorized searches of the colonial and Revolutionary era newspapers of other states.

In addition to promoting the preservation and publication of documents, the commission recognized the importance of preserving historic buildings. The first instance in which a state grant was given to a local, private, nonprofit institution for the preservation of a public building dates to 1908. The legislature assisted the Lincolnton United Daughters of the Confederacy (UDC) with the purchase of a building that once housed the Pleasant Retreat Academy, chartered in 1813 and opened in 1820. The UDC adapted the two-story Federal-style brick building for use as a museum of the Confederacy, a prospect that undoubtedly proved popular with veterans of the war then serving as members of the General Assembly.

2

The Teens: A Heightened Profile for the New Agency

The teens were a time of growth and development as the Historical Commission further defined its role in education, collection, and preservation. Only the third state historical agency in the nation, the commission had to forge policies and establish relationships with government agencies and the citizens as the new keeper of public memory. R. D. W. Connor sought advice and support from historians and archivists outside the state on several occasions and took an active role in professional conferences. Always the educator, Connor sought to build a Historical Commission that was public service oriented in order to make North Carolina's history accessible to all citizens.

The most obvious outward sign of growth during the teens was the physical move by the Historical Commission to offices in the new Administration Building on Morgan Street in 1914. A suite on the second floor offered the commission two large exhibition rooms for the Hall of History, three offices, two rooms for the conservation and mounting of documents, two rooms temporarily occupied by the State Library, a room for the storage of manuscripts, and a storage and shipping room. The fireproof facility was "equipped throughout with steel furniture." The new office space was seen as recognition for the increasingly important role of the Historical Commission in the state. Correspondingly, the additional chambers extended the commission's ability to serve the public as it rose to the challenges presented by its more visible position.

In 1912 R. D. W. Connor observed that genealogical inquiries were increasing every year and that the Historical Commission did not have enough staff to perform the requested research. Because Connor viewed genealogy as a method of disseminating knowledge related to North Carolina's history and resources, he anticipated assigning additional staff and space to such work once the agency was relocated to offices in the new Administration Building, planned for completion in 1914. He predicted, quite accurately, that genealogy "ought to become a source of considerable revenue to the Commission."

Working within the nascent archival program, Emily Taylor, employed in document restoration, was sent to the Library of Congress during the summer of 1911 to learn its methods for "repairing, mounting and filing of manuscripts." She

The state Administration Building as it appeared in the early 1910s. The North Carolina Historical Commission occupied the second floor from 1914 to 1939.

returned to the Historical Commission and performed much-needed conservation work on documents and volumes. In referring to the result of Taylor's work on the E. J. Hale Collection, which had been burned and damaged by water, Connor reported that "no damage whatever could be done to [the documents] by any reasonable use" following her repairs. After 1914 Taylor was given more space to perform conservation work in the Administration Building.

While North Carolina had its share of important persons and significant historical events and sites, few memorials existed to educate the public about them. Those which did exist had been privately purchased. As such, they could not rightly be considered to constitute part of the public memory of the state. The commission's initial involvement with memorials came at the State Capitol, where the group sought to fill all eight niches in the rotunda with busts of eminent North Carolinians. The first bust, that of William A. Graham, was unveiled in January 1910. Afterward the commission sought other appropriate figures to be similarly memorialized. In 1912 a resolution was passed that no bust, tablet, statue, or plaque would be placed in the Capitol without approval of the Historical Commission. In 1917 the General Assembly appropriated $2,500 per year for two years for use by the Historical Commission in placing markers at sites with historical significance—with a limit of $100 per marker, contingent on local matching funds. The first year of the program was indeed the most fruitful, with the commission granting almost the entire sum in portions ranging from $25 for a sign for a Tuscarora community in Bertie County to $500 for a group of twenty tablets along the Cape Fear River in New Hanover County.

The decade witnessed the Historical Commission's growth in both size and scope. In 1914 the General Assembly reassigned responsibility for the Hall of

Between 1917 and 1935 the North Carolina Historical Commission, in cooperation with local organizations, erected a number of bronze plaques throughout the state. This plaque in honor of Nathaniel Macon was placed in Warren County in 1919.

History from the Museum of Natural Sciences (in the Department of Agriculture) to the Historical Commission. With the museum collection came its curator and collector, Col. Fred Olds. Coinciding with Connor's late resolution to collect old records, the addition of Olds to the staff gave Connor the mechanism to seek out materials located throughout the state; in 1915 Olds toured selected counties, accomplishing that task. Between 1915 and 1916, nine counties surrendered old records to the Historical Commission, marking the beginning of the local records program. Colonel Olds's zeal for pursuing articles of material culture built a solid base for the museum's collection. Until his retirement in 1934, Olds kept an eye open and a hand outstretched for items he considered important for sharing North Carolina's story with the public.

The interior of the Hall of History in the state Administration Building.

Fred Olds: Father of the Museum of History

Frederick Augustus Olds, born in 1853, graduated from the Virginia Military Institute in 1872 and embarked upon a career in journalism. He served as city editor for the Raleigh *News and Observer* and kept a hand in the news business for four decades. Olds served in the State Guard and was appointed colonel (a title he would carry for life) on the staff of Gov. Zebulon B. Vance in 1877. By the mid-1880s, Olds had begun to collect materials as a consequence of a growing interest in North Carolina history. In 1902 the civic-minded Olds agreed to donate his large private collection to the state of North Carolina. His artifacts were merged with the state's meager collection of donated items and Olds became the collector of the expanded "Hall of History"—a position he cherished for the next thirty years.

Dissatisfaction with Olds appeared almost immediately. Stephen B. Weeks, a scholar hailed as North Carolina's first "professional" historian, complained in 1904 that Olds "brought Southern scholarship into the most well deserved contempt" and proclaimed Olds's work "a horrible example to be avoided." Yet Olds embraced his job with a passion held by few during that era. In 1914 the Hall of History came under the aegis of the North Carolina Historical Commission. Olds soon made his way to every county in the state in search of historical gems and the museum's holdings grew steadily. Unofficially, the dapper colonel assumed the mantle of "State Host" in Raleigh. Exuding warmth and charm, he gained a reputation for delighting thousands of tourists and schoolchildren in the Capital City. In declining health Olds retired in 1934 and died the following year at eighty-one.

Fred Olds (1853-1935), the father of the North Carolina Museum of History, posing in a Confederate uniform.

Over time it became fashionable for historians and museum professionals to disparage Olds and to snicker at his eccentric enthusiasm for North Carolina history. "Olds was a newspaper man," R. D. W. Connor said in a talk to Archives and History staff in 1948, "and he always looked at everything from a news point of view . . . [he was] very careless of his history." Nevertheless, it is important to remember that Olds was never officially recognized as a curator or historian and that he had no professional training. His title of "collector" for the Hall of History was an apt one, for it was Olds's unparalleled zeal in gathering objects related to the state's past that built the foundation of the present North Carolina Museum of History. In addition to thousands of artifacts, Olds collected many of the manuscripts that now reside in the State Archives.

Despite the lingering denigration of the man lauded in the *News and Observer* as North Carolina's "most useful, most popular, and most loved citizen," it must be acknowledged that no cadre of museum professionals existed in the late nineteenth and early twentieth centuries to build and expand the Hall of History. Overshadowing his role as "State Host," Fred Olds's enduring legacy dwells within the exhibits and sprawling storage facilities of the modern museum—a respected institution in which his core collection presently resides among enormously expanded holdings that now include more than 250,000 artifacts.—*Mark Anderson Moore*

From the outset of World War I, the Historical Commission collected materials, such as this poster, that were representative of the war effort in North Carolina. The 1919 legislature gave official sanction and financial support to the work.

Although both the State Archives and the Hall of History initiated the collection of war-related materials as soon as the United States entered World War I, the legislature of 1919 gave official sanction and financial support to the work. It was the desire of that body to put "into permanent and accessible form the history of the contribution of North Carolina and of her soldiers, sailors, airmen, and civilians to the Great World War while the records of those contributions are still available." The citizens of the state were quite interested in studying materials related to North Carolina's contributions to the war, and, as a consequence, the program received a great deal of publicity and volunteer assistance.

Four years earlier, in 1915, the General Assembly created the Legislative Reference Department and placed it under the control of the Historical Commission. The legislation authorized the Legislative Reference librarian "to collect, tabulate, annotate, and digest information for the use of the members and committees of the General Assembly, and other officials of the State, and of the various counties and cities included therein, upon all questions of state, county, and municipal legislation." It likewise empowered the librarian to assist with matters related to legislation in other states and nations and to keep various research materials on hand. The librarian was expected to arrange and classify all public bills and to answer any question posed by a legislator. The Legislative Reference Department remained a part of the Historical Commission until 1933, when it was moved to the Attorney General's Office.

3

The Twenties: Extending the Commission's Reach

The 1920s represent a period of successful implementation of the Historical Commission's prescribed duties. More secure with its status in the state, the commission staff made considerable progress with established programs while developing new ones. Although the leadership of the Historical Commission changed hands several times during the decade, the focus remained on the body's original mission, and the agency's influence extended farther than ever before.

The outreach of the Historical Commission during the twenties was largely a product of a publications initiative. In 1922 the commission issued the first volume of the widely acclaimed *Records of the Moravians in North Carolina*. The initial volume, translated and edited by Adelaide Fries, archivist of the Southern Province of the Moravian Church in America from 1911 to 1949, covers the period 1752 to 1771. Fries subsequently translated and edited six additional volumes in the series. The Moravian records not only document the activities of the church community but also function as a touchstone for the colony and state throughout its early history. By describing the events that affected both the church and the state and reflecting the concerns expressed by the leadership of both entities, the meticulously kept diaries, minutes, and correspondence represent an inestimable resource to the researcher of North Carolina history.

Taking its lead from other states, the Historical Commission resolved in 1922 to publish a state-supported quarterly magazine of scholarly historical articles and documents. The legislature appropriated money for the venture in 1923 and assigned Robert B. House, the collector of war records, the task of editing and otherwise preparing the journal under supervision of the secretary of the Historical Commission, then D. H. Hill Jr. Without so much as an idea for an article or even a name for the publication, House turned to R. D. W. Connor, whose counsel included the selection of a name: the *North Carolina Historical Review*.

When Hill died in 1924, House was named secretary of the commission, and he retained editorship of the *Review*. When House left at the end of 1925, he was succeeded by Albert Ray Newsome, the last person to hold the dual role of secretary of the Historical Commission and active editor of the *Review*. Newsome's background as a professional historian gave the journal the cushion of scholarly articles that it needed; indeed, in Newsome's nine years at the helm, he was the predominant contributor to the journal.

In June 1923 the Historical Commission became embroiled in a controversy. A proposal was floated to place the body within the Department of Public Instruction as the Bureau of Archives and History. Under the proposal, the commission would convert from being an autonomous agency appointed by the governor to an advisory body under the executive control of the superintendent of Public Instruction. In a flurry of activity, commission secretary Robert B. House wrote to historians and archivists, both within and outside the state, asking them for formal letters of support to preserve the commission's independent status. Many of those who responded to House viewed the proposal as potentially detrimental to the still-evolving Historical Commission, and the plans were discarded.

Robert B. House (1892-1987) was the first editor of the *North Carolina Historical Review* and secretary-treasurer of the North Carolina Historical Commission from 1920 to 1925.

In the 1920s the Historical Commission had not yet acquired title to any historic property in North Carolina, but two noteworthy events that transpired during that decade had implications for the agency's subsequent role as official caretaker of a variety of historic sites throughout the state. In 1923 the General Assembly created the Bennett Place Memorial Commission to accept custody of the land on which stood the homeplace of James and Nancy Bennitt, site of the April 1865 meeting between Union general William T. Sherman and Confederate general Joseph E. Johnston that effectively ended the Civil War, and to erect and maintain a unity monument there. The monument, which acknowledged the largest surrender of troops in the Civil War, was installed later that year. Moreover, in 1929 Mrs. William N. Reynolds, a wealthy philanthropist of Winston-Salem, made the first contribution to the restoration of the building known as Tryon Palace, the former New Bern residence of royal governor William Tryon. Ironically Mrs. Reynolds's gift, in the amount of $3,500, was placed in trust and never used for any actual restoration.

The Historical Commission acknowledged in May 1927 that "local history in North Carolina has not generally

The west wing of Tryon Palace, known as the Stable Office, is the only surviving part of the 1770 structure. Taken in the 1890s, this photograph shows the building when it served as an Episcopal parochial school.

The **North Carolina Historical Review:**
Seeking a Wider Audience for State History

From the first issue in January 1924, editors of the *North Carolina Historical Review* have placed a premium on sound scholarship, earning the quarterly its position among the foremost state history journals. Key to the *Review*'s development has been oversight by a board of respected professional historians and editorship by a succession of dedicated staff members. The journal's small circulation (1,512 in 2001) notwithstanding, the quarterly remains a foundation work for research in Tar Heel history. Hugh T. Lefler in 1952 estimated that one-third of *North Carolina: The History of a Southern State*, the textbook he coauthored with Albert Ray Newsome, was based on *Review* articles. A 1973 index to the *Review,* together with a 1983 supplement, remains the entry point for such research. An updated cumulative index is in preparation and will be made available online.

The success of the enterprise was not guaranteed. R. D. W. Connor in 1923 recognized the need (South Carolina, Tennessee, and Georgia already had such journals). Aside from Sunday newspapers, the *North Carolina Booklet*, issued by the Daughters of the American Revolution, was then the primary outlet for historical articles. Connor argued that "old hackneyed subjects" such as the "Mecklenburg Declaration of Independence" should be avoided. Considered initially as the title was *Quarterly Journal of the North Carolina Historical Commission.* Robert B. House, Connor's assistant (and subsequently successor), gathered for the initial issue a memorial address on Walter Hines Page, a World War diary, an essay on that war's bond campaign, a bibliography, book reviews, and historical news.

House assembled an editorial board in 1925, calling upon Greensboro professor Walter C. Jackson, Wilson educator Charles L. Coon, and Connor, the latter by then teaching history in Chapel Hill. Early and frequent contributors included J. G. de Roulhac Hamilton,

The
North Carolina
Historical
Review

ISSUED QUARTERLY

Volume I   Number 1

JANUARY, 1924

PUBLISHED BY
NORTH CAROLINA HISTORICAL COMMISSION
RALEIGH, N. C.

From the first issue in January 1924, editors of the *North Carolina Historical Review* have placed a premium on sound scholarship, earning the quarterly its position among the foremost state history journals.

had that systematic promotion which its importance deserves." In an effort to stimulate local historical activities, the commission advocated the selection of a county historian for each county, to be chosen by the local boards of education. Secretary Albert R. Newsome dispatched supporting letters to all chairmen of the county boards and published advertisements detailing the criteria for the county historians; the advertisements received wide circulation in the state's press. It was hoped that officially designated county historians would "stimulate local pride and achievement and add to the knowledge of North Carolina history." Specifically, the commission expected the county historian program to spawn such projects as the preparation of county cemetery surveys, the composition of historical articles for local newspapers, the location and preservation of historical manuscripts, suggestions of locations for historical markers, and the writing of definitive county histories.

By December 1927 county historians had been selected in about one-third of the counties, and within a year there were seventy-two. Although the historians were selected locally, many names were already familiar to the Historical

William K. Boyd, Adelaide L. Fries (the first woman, featured in the second issue), and Guion Griffis Johnson. John Hope Franklin in 1942 contributed articles on antebellum free blacks, and Dumas Malone and C. Vann Woodward were also published in the *Review*. Board members regularly rejected articles. Coon did not stint in his criticism: "It makes me weary and disgusted to read such unutterable drivel," he once wrote, calling another submission a "monstrous piece of asinine foolishness." In 1952 the board, inactive for several years, was revived. That body, presently composed of five members, remains central to the journal's operation. The editorial policy has retained a focus on North Carolina "and adjacent states," with a specific exclusion of material primarily genealogical in nature.

David Leroy Corbitt, hired as assistant editor in 1926, had primary responsibility for the *Review* through 1960. During his long tenure, Corbitt guided the quarterly through financial crises and periods during which submissions lagged (particularly during and after World War II). In 1952

David L. Corbitt (1895-1967) was hired as assistant editor of the *North Carolina Historical Review* in 1926. In 1936 he became managing editor and was responsible for the *Review* until 1960.

subscriptions were linked to membership in the Literary and Historical Association, thereby increasing circulation from 677 to 1,136. From that point until 1983, papers read at that group's annual meeting were reprinted in the *Review*. Corbitt's successors have included Memory F. Mitchell, Marie D. Moore, Jeffrey J. Crow, Joe A. Mobley, Kathleen B. Wyche, William A. Owens Jr., and Anne Miller.—*Michael Hill*

Commission. They included Charles L. Coon of Wilson County, Adelaide Fries of Forsyth County, M. C. S. Noble of Orange County, and Forster A. Sondley of Buncombe County. The work of the county historians was truly a labor of love, since there was no provision for payment and few counties had arrangements to reimburse their historians for travel expenses incurred in pursuit of their activities. In 1929 a member of the North Carolina General Assembly introduced a bill to make the title of county historian a paid position, but the state senate tabled the measure. The Historical Commission's involvement with the program faded by 1931. Among the accomplishments of the county historians in general were the creation of local historical societies and the stimulation of general interest in history. The commission's stated goal of generating published county histories remained largely unfulfilled, however. The officially sanctioned county historians completed published histories for eleven counties, and the historian of New Hanover County completed a two-volume work.

During the 1920s the Historical Commission authorized two projects involving the publication of North Carolina-related records held by foreign repositories.

Irene Wright (*center*) transcribing records in the Archives of the Indies in Seville, Spain, in November 1925. Between 1922 and 1926, researchers investigated and copied North Carolina-related records in archives in England and Spain.

R. D. W. Connor spent the summer of 1922 in England examining materials at the British Public Records Office and the British Museum. His work was considered to be urgent, inasmuch as the documents in question were in poor condition, but Connor spent most of his time attempting to identify the most important records related to North Carolina and learning how to obtain copies of those items. In April 1924 the Historical Commission authorized Prof. W. W. Pierson of the University of North Carolina to investigate public records in Spain as Connor had done in England. Pierson found "an astonishingly large collection of hitherto unused material vitally pertinent to North Carolina history from the middle of the sixteenth through the first years of the nineteenth century, much of which was in a bad state of preservation." He encountered a wealth of material in the National Historical Archives at Madrid and employed a copyist there. An even larger collection of materials related to subjects of interest to North Carolinians was located in the General Archives of the Indies in Seville. There Pierson engaged Irene Wright to make photostatic copies. When he found yet more material in the archives at Simancas, he hired a copyist there as well. The copying of these records continued until July 1926, when the funding for the project ran out. Additional funds were secured a year later, but within a few weeks of the resumption of the project the king of Spain declared that full series of Spanish records could no longer be copied. Despite appeals from the Historical Commission and other repositories in the United States, the restriction remained in effect. Prior to the king's action, the Historical Commission had secured a total of 15,120 pages of photostats and 1,512 pages of typescripts ranging from 1566 to 1800.

4

The Thirties: Eclipsed by Federal Projects

Despite extensive economic hardship throughout the nation, the North Carolina Historical Commission managed to survive, and in fact to thrive, during the 1930s. The agency operated under a greatly reduced budget for nearly the entire decade. Appropriations reached a low of $11,315 in 1934-1935, about one-third of the operating budget prior to the depression. In spite of that impediment, the commission managed to remain intact and even to make progress. Federal-aid projects helped it accomplish its goals by providing workers and resources, and favorable state legislation augmented its power and enhanced its credibility as the state's historical agency.

The one program within the Historical Commission that was significantly limited by the economic crisis was that of publications. During the 1932-1934 biennium the publishing of documentary volumes was discontinued, only to resume briefly in 1935 when the third volume of *The Papers of Randolph Abbott Shotwell* went to press. That book was not actually published until 1936. Besides a few small pamphlets, biennial reports, and the *North Carolina Historical Review*, only Works Progress Administration (WPA)-supported publications were produced for the remainder of the 1930s. Among the most significant WPA works published during the decade were comprehensive surveys of public records in each county. The WPA completed the task of inspecting and recording all county records—a project that had long been an unattainable goal of the commission—and published it in three volumes, arranged alphabetically by county name, in 1938 and 1939.

The Historical Commission had a successful year with the General Assembly in 1935. The Public Records Act of that year was Albert R. Newsome's crowning achievement during his tenure as secretary. He had begun his campaign for such legislation in 1932. The legislation was the state's first comprehensive legal action designed to protect and preserve public records. Chapter 265, "An Act to Safeguard Public Records in North Carolina," defined public records, assigned accountability for their care, and prohibited the sale, loan, or destruction of records without the consent of the Historical Commission. In addition, the act required public officials to deliver all public records from their term of office to their

The Historical Records Survey: A WPA Project in the Service of Research

The Works Progress Administration (WPA), the massive New Deal program devised to employ those down on their luck, extended its reach to white-collar workers through various literary and historical programs. Perhaps the most noteworthy of WPA efforts was the Federal Writers' Project, rightly renowned in the Tar Heel State for the 1939 volumes *North Carolina: A Guide to the Old North State* and *These Are Our Lives*. Of greatest consequence to the work of the Historical Commission, and in particular the archival management program, was the Historical Records Survey.

The objective of the survey was the "discovery, preservation, and listing of basic materials for research in the history of the United States." The first task was to inventory and list all state, county, and municipal records. "The sheer size of the task might have staggered men of fainter heart," the survey's state director, Christopher Crittenden, later recalled. As a result, the Historical Commission formulated a long-term county records management program, part of its core mission today.

Crittenden assembled a board of scholars as advisers and hired as an assistant Dan M. Lacy, a twenty-two-year-old history instructor in Chapel Hill. The two men began work in February 1936, employing as many as 130 workers during the first year. Administrators, who reduced the paperwork to a minimum and simplified the forms, nevertheless found it difficult to locate skilled workers. Federal regulations limited the number of nonrelief workers to only 25 percent (a number later reduced to 5 percent) of the survey team. From field offices in eight cities, workers combed courthouse basements and city hall attics throughout the state, often encountering local officials with proprietary attitudes about their records and a reluctance to permit the survey team to do its work.

North Carolina became the first state to publish a survey and the only one to publish guides to all of its county records. *The Historical Records of North Carolina* appeared in three volumes in 1938 and 1939. Copies were supplied to all of the state's courthouses and to many libraries throughout the nation. Postcards announcing the volumes went out with the promise of copies in exchange for 25 cents to cover postage. Critical reaction was positive. Historian Richard Morris wrote that the published volumes "set a standard for all other state projects." "That this work will be useful cannot be doubted," a writer for the *Baltimore Sun* editorialized.

The Chowan County Courthouse, circa 1932. WPA workers inventoried local records at this and other courthouses throughout North Carolina as part of the Historical Records Survey.

The work of the survey did not end with the three volumes. As canvasses of the county records were completed, relief workers moved on to record tombstone inscriptions, covering more than 140,000 people and 4,500 cemeteries. Work proceeded on a catalog of early American imprints and on inventories of manuscripts in the Southern Historical Collection, the Duke University Library, and the State Archives, as well as in Moravian and Presbyterian archives. Lacy resigned in April 1940, and the project was shuttered in the summer of 1942 as the nation geared up for war. The sum total of the work of the Historical Records Survey proved of inestimable value to future generations of archivists and researchers.—*Michael Hill*

successors; provided for the mandatory return of public records found out of custody; and required officials to provide access to records and make copies readily available to the public on demand. During the same session, the General Assembly enacted Chapter 300, "An Act to Protect the Property of the Public Libraries and Other Agencies from Malicious Injury." That legislation, which encompassed books, periodicals, maps, public records, pictures, and any other item belonging to a public library, museum, public office, or educational institution, made it illegal to steal, damage, sell, or receive any of those materials. The offender would be charged with a misdemeanor if the value of the item in question was under twenty dollars and a felony if it was valued at more than that amount. The legislation offered important increased legal protection to the records of North Carolina and further strengthened the ability of the Historical Commission to act on behalf of preserving those records.

The 1935 General Assembly also appropriated five thousand dollars per year for each of the ensuing three years to enable the Highway and Public Works Commission to erect highway historical markers in North Carolina. Although the highway marker program began as a joint project of the Highway and Public Works Commission, the Department of Conservation and Development, and the Historical Commission, the collector of the Hall of History was initially assigned responsibility for conducting all research involved in marker proposals. The state was divided into seventeen districts and each district was assigned a letter from A to Q; then each marker was given a number in conjunction with the letter for its district. Thus each marker would have an identifying code. The first marker erected (on January 10, 1935) was G-1, which designated the former

home of John Penn, a North Carolina signer of the Declaration of Independence. The legislation further provided for an advisory committee to be made up of college or university professors. (At the present time that committee is comprised of ten faculty members who are experts in North Carolina history and who teach at four-year colleges or universities. They are appointed by the secretary of Cultural Resources to serve five-year terms. All proposed markers erected must meet the committee's approval before they can be erected.)

Although prehistory was of cursory interest to the Historical Commission at the time, the mid-1930s were an important period for the archaeological community in North Carolina. Archaeologists from throughout the state formed the Archaeological Society of

This marker in Dare County dedicated to the Roanoke colonies was among the first five signs approved by the North Carolina Highway Historical Marker Advisory Committee in 1935.

Town Creek Indian Mound and North Carolina Archaeology

In 1936, after dealing with trespassers and artifact hunters for years, Lloyd Frutchey decided to flatten the odd, purportedly Indian, embankment on his property in Montgomery County. He planned to use the soil to bolster eroded plots on his farm. Members of North Carolina's budding archaeological community learned of Frutchey's plans and enlisted Christopher Crittenden's help in trying to protect the area. In January 1937 a small delegation, including state officials and an archaeologist, evaluated the mound and approached Frutchey with ideas for preserving it. Following negotiations, it was agreed that Frutchey would deed the mound and a small amount of surrounding land to the state, specifically the Department of Conservation and Development, which would administer the site and care for the artifacts found there. The area was known as Frutchey State Park, or the Frutchey mound, until the 1940s, when its name was changed to Town Creek, after a nearby rivulet.

Funds were hard to come by during the early years of excavation at the site.

The excavation of the Frutchey mound at Town Creek. The site, seen here in the late 1930s, was the first major archaeological project involving the Historical Commission.

North Carolina in 1933. As a result of efforts on the part of the society, the legislature in 1935 enacted a comprehensive "Indian Antiquities Law," which for the first time recognized the historical and scientific value of prehistoric remains. The law encouraged citizens to turn over Indian artifacts to the Historical Commission and made it a misdemeanor to destroy or sell relics found on state property. The Town Creek Indian Mound in Montgomery County—a prehistory site that had been investigated, and even occasionally plundered, by both amateurs and professionals for years—came to the attention of the Historical Commission in 1936. The owner of the property on which the mound stood had grown weary of trespassers and curious relic hunters on his land and resolved that he would level the mound to improve nearby farmland. The Archaeological Society of North Carolina, the Historical Commission, and various other interested parties clamored to save the mound and, in doing so, created a state park and acquired an archaeological excavation that was quickly approved as a WPA work project. A young archaeologist from the University of North Carolina named Joffre Coe was chosen to supervise the effort.

WPA projects of the 1930s and early 1940s, which provided work for many unemployed North Carolinians, also made significant contributions to the goals of the Historical Commission. WPA projects such as the county records surveys, the

It now seems quite fortunate that money was not available to develop the site according to early State Parks plans. If funds had been available, much of what is now excavated at Town Creek might have been destroyed by the construction of a large parking lot. In November 1939 excavations at Town Creek were approved as a Works Progress Administration (WPA) project. Some of the best archaeological work performed at the site was completed during the WPA years. The United States' involvement in World War II effectively put an end to all WPA projects; Town Creek excavations were discontinued until 1949.

Upon his return from military service in 1946, Joffre Coe visited Town Creek to inspect for pillaging or damage and then went directly to Chapel Hill to set up the university's archaeological lab, which for years thereafter served as the repository for all of the state's archaeological relics. Coe, the archaeological supervisor of Town Creek beginning in 1937, continued in that capacity for more than fifty years. Between 1950 and 1951 the state acquired fifty-two additional acres of land around the original site. At the time, plans were advanced for restoring the mound and palisade, reconstructing a town house on the mound, and interpreting the site through permanent museum exhibits.

Town Creek Indian Mound became a part of what was then the Department of Archives and History's new Division of Historic Sites in 1955. By that time the mound had been restored and the stockade around the original site had been reconstructed. The site received electrical power in 1960, at which time a manager's house was begun; an access road was paved in 1962. Town Creek was designated as a National Historic Landmark in 1965. Additional pre-Columbian facilities reconstructed at the site include a major and a minor temple, a burial hut, and a mortuary hut. A learning center, built in 1991 to increase educational and interpretive opportunities, offers space for demonstrations of Native American skills and crafts.—*Ansley Herring Wegner*

---

indexing of marriage bonds, the *State* magazine, *Moore's Roster* of Confederate soldiers, and the card catalog and carbon typescripts of pre–1913 tombstones represent work that could never have been completed with the staff and budget of the Historical Commission at the time. Indeed, the budget for WPA programs was far greater than that of the Historical Commission. In the 1936-1938 biennium, for example, the WPA budget for programs conducted in conjunction with the commission was approximately two hundred thousand dollars, or about five times the commission's budget for those years. Moreover, the manpower provided by the federal projects could never have been matched by state agencies.

Another WPA project that ended up involving the Historical Commission was construction of replica buildings at the presumed site of Fort Raleigh on Roanoke Island. In order to utilize federal funds for the venture, the Historical Commission was obliged to assume ownership of the site from the Roanoke Colony Memorial Association, which had owned the property since 1894. The commission was unable to obtain the state funding necessary for maintenance and administration of the site, however, and therefore offered it to the National Park Service in 1936. That agency accepted the offer in 1938 and developed the site as part of the national park system. Amidst the negotiations over the site, the year 1937 saw the 350th anniversary celebration of the Roanoke voyages and the premier of Paul Green's outdoor drama *The Lost Colony*.

Gertrude Carraway (1896-1993), preservationist, historian, and journalist. She served as a member of the North Carolina Historical Commission from 1942 to 1983 and was an honorary member until her death. She was instrumental in the restoration of Tryon Palace, serving as secretary of the Tryon Palace Commission from 1945 to 1971.

Three events in 1939 ranked low on the Historical Commission's agenda at the time but came to be seen as important in later years. First, original plans for Tryon Palace were located at the New-York Historical Society in the papers of Francis Lister Hawks, the grandson of palace architect John Hawks. A more complete set was discovered at the British Public Record Office (PRO), and still others were found in the Library of Congress. Gertrude Carraway, a newspaper writer of New Bern, aided by Christopher Crittenden, had begun searching for palace plans in 1937. Their work met with bountiful success in two years' time. The discovery of the plans stimulated activity and discussions related to excavation and restoration of the palace. In December 1939 the excavation of Tryon Palace was approved as a WPA archaeological project.

Also in 1939, the state contracted with the federal government for a ninety-nine-year lease on the planter's house and the seven remaining outbuildings at the former Somerset Plantation near Lake Phelps to create a state park. The original buildings were incorporated into the boundaries of the newly formed Pettigrew State Park. The structures and the immediate grounds were acquired through a quitclaim deed in 1947, and the area was designated a state historic site in 1969.

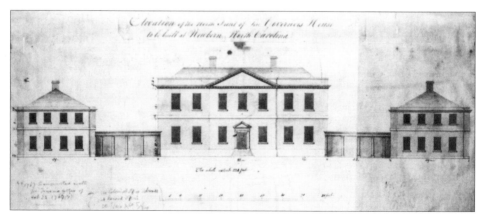

The original plans of Tryon Palace were discovered at the New-York Historical Society in the papers of Francis Lister Hawks, the grandson of palace architect John Hawks.

Chapter Four

Christopher Crittenden: Populist Historian at the Helm

A generation after Christopher Crittenden's death, his contributions continue to inspire his successors at Archives and History. Given his long tenure at the agency, the role he played in developing state programs, and the leadership he offered to national historical organizations, it is unlikely that those who come after will leave as indelible an imprint.

Christopher Crittenden, born on December 1, 1902, maintained lifelong ties to Wake Forest College, where his father was a teacher and his mother a librarian. His maternal grandfather had been the school's president. He earned bachelor's and master's degrees from Wake Forest and a doctorate at Yale University in 1930. His dissertation became his second book, *The Commerce of North Carolina, 1763-1789*, published in 1936. His first book was *North Carolina Newspapers before 1790* (1928). Crittenden taught history at Yale while completing his studies and from 1930 to 1935 was an assistant professor in Chapel Hill.

On July 1, 1935, Crittenden replaced Albert Ray Newsome as secretary of the North Carolina Historical Commission, beginning a thirty-four-year association with the state office. During that time the agency increased in size from 8 to 135 employees. Davidson College professor Frontis Johnston once remarked that Crittenden was "a giant among state historical leaders and more than anyone else gave the North Carolina agency a national reputation." Crittenden's successor as director, H. G. Jones, declared that the tall, bald-headed, bow-tied historian loved practical jokes and "burgeoned out the best in his staff."

During Crittenden's tenure the agency spearheaded the highway historical marker program, extended its publications offerings, pioneered modern records management, began a system of state-owned historic sites, and launched modern museum and preservation programs. The marker program, an initiative he inherited from Newsome, exemplified his philosophy of "history for all the people." Crittenden attended hundreds of programs across the state, regularly distributed press releases, and became the public face of Archives and History. While maintaining high professional standards and a close working relationship with academics, he demonstrated that history was not solely the province of the ivory tower.

Crittenden served, at the state level, as secretary of the Literary and Historical Association (promoting in particular the annual gathering that came to be known as "Culture Week") and headed commemorations of anniversaries of the Carolina

Christopher Crittenden (1902-1969) and his wife, Janet, in Wilmington in 1930. They were married on September 6, 1930.

Charter and the Civil War. On the national level, he was the first president of the American Association for State and Local History (1940-1942) and president of the Society of American Archivists (1946-1948). He received honorary doctorates from Wake Forest University and the University of North Carolina at Chapel Hill. In 1968, the year the agency occupied its present building, Crittenden stepped down to serve as assistant director. Just before entering the hospital three weeks before his death on October 13, 1969, he left in his desk a note offering suggestions regarding his funeral. "Kindly have the doctor double check to make absolutely certain that I am dead," he instructed, closing "Good luck to everybody."—*Michael Hill*

The North Carolina Society for the Preservation of Antiquities and the Modern Preservation Movement

In 1938 the Garden Club of North Carolina hosted a "Garden Fortnight and Tour" in order to "stimulate interest in the historic treasures of North Carolina." Janie Fetner Gosney of Raleigh directed the tour. Fueled by the success of the endeavor, the group formed a restoration committee and resolved to produce a book. A limited-edition volume titled *Old Homes and Gardens of North Carolina*, with text by Archibald Henderson and photographs by Bayard Wootten, appeared in 1939. The volume, in keeping with the popular assessment of preservationists at the time, featured primarily the most magnificent examples. It was with the preservation of such grand structures in mind, of

Members of the Society for the Preservation of Antiquities conducted their first board meeting in December 193? Pictured here at that meeting are, from left to right: Margaret Smethurst; Christopher Crittenden; Adelaide Fries; Joseph Hyde Pratt, president; Janie Fetner Gosney; Ruth Coltrane Cannon; and Emily Gilliam Gary.

In still another important undertaking in 1939, Secretary Christopher Crittenden was instrumental in the formation of the North Carolina Society for the Preservation of Antiquities. Indeed, the society maintained office space within the commission's headquarters, and Crittenden was named an ex officio member of its board. The society remained a private venture but was influential in the evolution of state historic preservation initiatives.

The State Archives' manuscript filing room and the Hall of History display areas had become full by 1930. The office space acquired by the Historical Commission just sixteen years earlier had become inadequate. As mentioned previously, the Historical Commission fared well with the General Assembly during the 1930s. Nowhere is this more evident than in the 1937 appropriation of $675,000 for a new Education Building in which the Historical Commission would occupy the entire first floor and half of the basement. The new facility, occupied in 1939, enabled more researchers to utilize the State Archives Search Room; more visitors to tour the Hall of History; and allowed additional space

which there were ever fewer remaining, that the clubwomen set out to form a preservation organization. Maude Moore Latham, a noted Greensboro philanthropist, contemplated the charge in a letter to restoration committee chair Ruth Coltrane Cannon. Latham wrote that "we should have at least a place in every county but [I] am not at all certain that every county has one place of interest."

With the Historical Commission financially incapable of acquiring and restoring historic properties, Secretary Christopher Crittenden included a plea for the creation of a private preservation organization in his 1936-1938 biennial report. Shortly thereafter, Crittenden wrote that "the Society . . . should be headed by a man, but most of the actual work should be done by a woman, who would be called Executive Vice-President, or something of the sort." Gosney was selected to manage the nascent group, with the title of secretary-treasurer. The first president was Joseph Hyde Pratt, former state geologist, who was influential in many state and national associations. With the encouragement and support of the Garden Club and the Literary and Historical Association, the North Carolina Society for the Preservation of Antiquities was formed in 1939. Crittenden was instrumental in the effort; the group kept an office in the Historical Commission suite. Cannon served as the society's president from 1944 to 1956 and is credited with rescuing the group from an imminent demise. The group still awards the Cannon Cup to people and organizations active in historic preservation.

In 1974 the North Carolina Society for the Preservation of Antiquities was rechartered as the Historic Preservation Society of North Carolina. The society established a revolving preservation fund to purchase and resell endangered historic properties. The fund and the society merged in 1984, at which point the organization was called the Historic Preservation Foundation. The group, presently known as Preservation North Carolina (PNC), maintains the revolving fund that has assisted in the rehabilitation of numerous structures representing the broad patterns of the state's history and its architectural resources, including the Briggs Hardware building in Raleigh, the Bellamy Mansion in Wilmington, and the Edenton Mill Village. Preservation North Carolina and the State Historic Preservation Office conduct very different but mutually sustaining programs. PNC also engages in political advocacy on behalf of historic preservation.—*Ansley Herring Wegner*

for storage, processing, and conservation, further enhancing the stature of the Historical Commission.

The Education Building, home to the North Carolina Historical Commission and the Hall of History from 1939 to 1969.

5

The Forties: Commission to Department

The 1940s were a time of adaptation to external changes. The Historical Commission adjusted to war and to the consequences of war, to more readily available micrographics technology, and to wider participation by other organizations in the preservation of North Carolina's history. Although the productive WPA projects came to an end because of the war, the Historical Commission extended its existing services and launched new initiatives.

Just before the war and the resulting disbanding of federal projects, the Historical Commission, the WPA, and the Genealogical Society of Utah (Mormon Church) entered into an agreement that allowed the Genealogical Society to microfilm North Carolina's public records. The Genealogical Society agreed to supply the camera, materials, and camera operator and to send copies of all materials filmed at the county courthouses to the Historical Commission, as well as to Utah. The WPA was to supply the workers to prepare materials for filming; the commission permitted the filming of its records on-site and assisted with arrangements at the county level. The WPA's untimely subsequent withdrawal forced the Historical Commission to provide all of the preparatory work. Filming began at the Historical Commission offices in May 1941 and in the counties the following November. While initial output was high, problems arose with the equipment, resulting in the abandonment of the project until after the war. Filming did not resume in earnest until 1949.

Prior to that joint effort, the Historical Commission had no microfilm in its collection. Microfilming for records management purposes was just starting to become popular in government agencies in advance of the war. The U.S. Department of Agriculture and the U.S. Navy had just begun microfilming noncurrent records, and the army was exploring the benefits of the technology. The momentum behind security microfilming of records accelerated during the war. Filming was popular because it generated copies of records in a space-saving, convenient format at a relatively low cost. Further augmenting the nontextual collections of the Historical Commission in 1942 was the addition of the Raleigh *News and Observer* photographic negatives. At the time, staff members predicted that the collection would be "increasingly valuable and important as the years

Herb Paschal filing a roll of microfilm. In 1941, the Historical Commission began filming North Carolina's public records. The agency purchased its own flatbed microfilm camera and darkroom in 1949. Paschal, later a history professor at East Carolina University, was hired in 1951.

pass." Indeed this was a prophetic statement. With thousands of negatives, the *News and Observer* collection documents life in the state from 1938 to 1989 and is used by researchers daily.

The General Assembly passed a bill in 1943 changing the name of the Historical Commission to the State Department of Archives and History. The change came at the request of Christopher Crittenden and the commission, whose members believed that the new designation better emphasized the work and the importance of the agency. In 1945 the title of secretary was changed to director. The governing board (which likewise had been known as the Historical Commission), consisting of seven members since 1941 rather than the original five, became the Executive Board of Archives and History.

The war had profound consequences for the Historical Commission. Even before the nation's involvement in combat, the Hall of History was conducting studies to determine how to adapt to wartime conditions such as air raids. Staff members investigated plans for transporting valuable items from the State Archives and the Hall of History to safe depositories, if necessary, but the humidity and other environmental hazards of inappropriate storage made such an evacuation unlikely. Indeed, at a meeting of the North Carolina State Committee on Conservation of Cultural Resources in 1942, R. D. W. Connor noted that civilian morale would be better served by keeping cultural institutions open. The committee, comprised of historians, archivists, and librarians from across the state, continued to meet throughout the war to discuss the protection of the state's cultural heritage.

In 1941 Christopher Crittenden wrote prophetically: "In time of war the nation needs more than ever to preserve its traditions and ideals, lest in the supreme effort of winning a war we forget and lose the very things we seek to preserve." The Hall of History took Crittenden's statement to heart. Its display areas were kept open Saturday and Sunday afternoons and on holidays prior to and throughout the war to give families, servicemen, and other war workers an enjoyable diversion. The exhibits were carefully designed to boost morale. One of the more interesting ventures was an art restoration shop set up in the fall of 1943 so that visitors to the Hall of History could watch Arthur Edwin Bye, a

A store front in Kinston houses a display of captured war trophies owned by a local soldier. The photo was sent to the State Archives with a description of each item as part of the Lenoir County World War II collection.

portrait restorer, attend to portraits in the collection. Bye was commissioned to restore thirty-five portraits from the collection. Exhibited for the first time during the war years was the collection of gowns worn by the governors' wives. It would prove to be one of the museum's evergreens. The Hall of History's first acquisition for the display was Mrs. Alice Broughton's inaugural gown, worn at that event in 1941. At the close of the war, there was an exhibit of Japanese weaponry captured during the war by the 81st Infantry, or "Wildcat Division," a unit comprised primarily of North Carolinians.

With precedents established by the collection of World War I records, the acquisition of materials related to World War II commenced in February 1942. Given no appropriation for the program, the Historical Commission made adjustments in staff responsibilities in order to assign a person to the project fulltime. Gov. J. Melville Broughton asked the 1943 General Assembly to support the war records program and, accordingly, the needed funds were made available at midyear. People throughout the state, including educators and members of local governments, chambers of commerce, and patriotic organizations, offered assistance. Official collectors were designated in most counties. Performing the collecting duties on a volunteer basis, those citizens maintained other jobs, with many lawyers, teachers, and journalists participating. Historian John Hope Franklin helped collect war records related to African Americans. Overall, the efforts to collect and preserve the war records brought positive attention to the agency.

A collection of captured Nazi and Japanese weapons displayed in the Modern War Room of the Hall of History during World War II.

Another activity begun during wartime that drew the public eye was a weekly newspaper column written by Christopher Crittenden, with the occasional assistance of his colleagues. The feature, called *In Light of History*, consisted of articles designed to present the historical background behind topics of contemporary interest, such as the observance of Labor Day or the payment of income taxes. The column, distributed by the Associated Press, ran in newspapers in North Carolina, South Carolina, Virginia, Georgia, Florida, and Alabama. It was so popular that the director of Archives and History continued to write the essays for many years. Employees of the department conducted research and wrote historical sketches on North Carolinians such as Virginia Dare and Hugh Williamson for consideration in the naming of Liberty Ships. At the North Carolina Shipbuilding Company in Wilmington, 126 such vessels were constructed; many bore the names of people important to the state's history.

Despite the money made available for the war-related functions, other efforts of the department suffered. For lack of funds, documentary volumes were discontinued again, this time between 1943 and 1946, and the highway historical marker program was suspended from 1942 to 1947 because of metal shortages. When the marker program was reinstated, the contract to produce them went to Sewah Studios in Ohio (which began employing lowercase lettering in place of the solid capitals used on prewar markers). Sewah remains the supplier for historical markers to the present.

In keeping with the micrographics work launched in 1941 and the agreement with the Genealogical Society of Utah, the Department of Archives and History began purchasing microfilm from the federal government in the 1944-1946 biennium. The first such acquisition was forty-three reels of film covering the censuses of 1830 through 1870. Although the State Archives had paper copies of some of the census material (received from the Secretary of State's Office in the 1920s), the originals were tattered from years of use and were incomplete, with some lacking enumerator's districts and some counties missing altogether. The substitution of the federal microfilm provided researchers with better records and made possible the preservation of the originals. With the ever-increasing number of genealogists in mind, the State Archives sought to make county records, especially those in bound volumes, available on microfilm in the Search Room. By the end of the 1944-1946 biennium, and with the help of the Genealogical Society of Utah, the department had on hand 738 reels of county records on microfilm.

As gasoline rationing was lifted at the close of the war and travelers took to the road, the use of the Search Room increased as well. The convenience of having the newly microfilmed federal census records and county records available in Raleigh drew genealogists from all over North Carolina and from around the country. Indeed, the number of researchers from outside of the state doubled that of the wartime years.

With the North Carolina Society for the Preservation of Antiquities (having been organized in 1939) taking hold, historic preservation gained the attention of the department, as well as the public. Although not yet a part of the agency, Tryon Palace was of great interest to the staff. In January 1941 Maude Moore Latham, a Greensboro resident but native of New Bern, established a trust fund with a gift of $100,000 in stock to be used to restore the palace, contingent on the state's acquiring the palace site and maintaining and operating the restored property. Despite much controversy, a bill to appropriate $150,000 for the purchase of the site as a state park passed both houses of the General Assembly in February 1945. A separate measure established the Tryon Palace Commission to oversee the restoration and to manage the property upon completion. Christopher Crittenden was an ex officio member of that group.

North Carolina's first local historic preservation ordinance was adopted in Winston-Salem in 1948. The ordinance was designed to protect the site of the 1766 Moravian community of Salem (present-day Old Salem) from encroaching development. Two years later a nonprofit organization was chartered to preserve, restore, and interpret the site as a living history community. Legislation enacted by the General Assembly in 1965 gave Winston-Salem the authority to establish the Old Salem Historic District and a local governing commission and also authorized a few other towns to establish historic districts. The law, a turning point for historic preservation in North Carolina, was rewritten in 1971 to enable all local governments to establish historic districts and historic landmarks commissions. Local property tax deferrals for locally designated historic landmarks, initiated in 1975, further boosted preservation efforts.

Tryon Palace: North Carolina's Colonial Capitol

Maude Moore Latham (1871-1951), philanthropist and benefactor, established a trust fund to pay for the restoration of Tryon Palace.

Tryon Palace, New Bern's glorious mansion and seat of the colonial government during the tenures of North Carolina's last two royal governors, was constructed between 1767 and 1770. Architect John Hawks designed what was considered to be one of the grandest structures in British North America. The estate was the site of the First Provincial Congress in 1774 and the first meeting of the state's legislature in 1777. With the new state government meeting in various locations prior to the establishment of the permanent capital in Raleigh, Tryon Palace began to deteriorate from indifference and neglect. In 1791 George Washington described it as "a good brick building but now hastening to ruin." A fire destroyed the main section in 1798, but the two wings were saved. While the East Wing's fate is unknown, the West Wing served many functions over the years until it landed in the hands of the state of North Carolina again nearly 150 years later.

As early as 1926, citizens of New Bern talked of reconstructing Tryon Palace, and no one talked of it more loudly than did local newspaperwoman Gertrude Carraway; but the movement did not begin in earnest until January 1944. At that time philanthropist Maude Moore Latham, a Greensboro resident but native of New Bern, established a trust fund with a gift of $100,000 in stock to be used for the restoration. Her gift was contingent on the purchase of the palace site and the maintenance and operation of the restored property by the state. Christopher Crittenden was named to the board of trustees of the trust fund. The Executive Board of the Department, formerly the Historical Commission, passed a resolution supporting the state's involvement in the project.

Following a visit to Williamsburg, Virginia, Gov. J. Melville Broughton was convinced that the restoration would bring large numbers of tourists into the state. In fact, a Williamsburg official jokingly offered to personally finance the whole project if he could have in return the gasoline taxes paid by tourists to the site. The Department of Archives and History published and distributed an eighteen-page pamphlet about Tryon Palace, written by Gertrude Carraway, to enlighten legislators and other citizens about the historical significance of the building. With the help of such shows of support, legislation was adopted in February 1945 appropriating $150,000 for the project. Maude Moore Latham died in 1951, leaving the residue of her estate, then valued at $1,116,000, to the Tryon Palace Commission to ensure the complete restoration of the palace—her life's dream.

In January 1952 William G. Perry, a Boston architect, was selected to draft the plans for the palace. His experience with the reconstruction at Williamsburg made him uniquely qualified for the project. By that time Maude Moore Latham's daughter, May Gordon Latham Kellenberger, chaired the Tryon Palace Commission. Mrs. Kellenberger and her husband John in turn devoted their time and resources to the restoration and development of the complex through the auspices of their own legacy, the Kellenberger Historical Foundation of New Bern. Tryon Palace, which opened to the public on April 10, 1959, is presently a jewel in the crown of Archives and History and annually receives in excess of 85,000 visitors.—*Ansley Herring Wegner*

Joye Jordan was hired in 1945 to head the newly created museum division, with the understanding she would step down when the men returned from World War II. Nevertheless, she retained that position for almost three decades.

So many men were off fighting in the war in 1945 that Christopher Crittenden hired Joye Jordan as head of the newly created museum division—with the understanding that when the men came back home, she would step down. After all, Crittenden believed that the position was "a man's job." Jordan, of course, did not vacate the position until she was promoted to assistant director of Archives and History in 1972. Upon assuming her position in 1945, Jordan resumed the accessioning and cataloging of items initially begun in the mid-1930s by J. Carlyle Sitterson, then a graduate student at the University of North Carolina. The completion of a thorough inventory took two years but resulted in a comprehensive catalog. The inventory also brought to light various storage problems. Special storage cases were installed for items such as guns, swords, and costumes. Upon completion of the inventory, Jordan introduced the notion of defining a collection policy. The Hall of History became more selective with its accessions, no longer accepting any item offered.

One of the most important additions to Archives and History's collections came in 1949. The Carolina Charter of 1663 had been offered for sale by an antiquarian bookseller in England in 1947. The department and the Executive Board immediately began to investigate the authenticity of the document. The bookseller was cooperative and agreed to send the Charter to state officials on approval so that its authenticity could be verified by American experts. Indeed, exhaustive research was conducted on both sides of the Atlantic. While the document itself was being examined in the United States, its provenance, or chain of ownership, was being traced in England. The research indicated that the document was authentic. The bookseller, in a show of goodwill, reduced the asking price of £2,500 to £2,000 ($10,000 to $6,000), so long as the document was purchased by or given to the state of North Carolina. A legislative appropriation in 1951 provided for the construction of a custom-made fireproof display case for the Charter. (While the Charter had been accessioned by the State Archives, it was displayed by the Hall of History/Museum of History in the Education Building and in the new Archives and History/State Library Building until the museum moved to its own building in the 1990s.)

The Carolina Charter of 1663 (*portion*). The Charter was purchased in 1949 from an antiquarian bookseller in England for the sum of $6,000.

In 1945 the General Assembly enacted legislation to "redefine and clarify the duties and functions" of the Department of Archives and History. A primary concern was prevention of the unauthorized destruction of records and the establishment of safeguards against the accidental disposal of permanently valuable records. By 1949 the department was involved in records management in earnest. Records managers and archivists were engaged in developing plans and making recommendations for the retirement or disposal of state agency and county records. A makeshift records center for the storage of semicurrent state agency records had been situated in the department's warehouse at the State Fairgrounds. In July 1949 the department purchased a flatbed microfilm camera and set up a darkroom within the departmental offices so that security microfilm could be easily prepared on-site. The New Deal, the World Wars, and increased government involvement in regulatory and social programs caused a tremendous expansion in records creation. Administrators of the Department of Archives and History realized that the daunting but essential task of dealing with public records would fall to them. No longer could the agency focus only on preserving old records of historical value to researchers; it now had to tame the modern paper tiger—the records of a modern and expanding government.

6

The Fifties: Historic Sites Find a Home

In 1955, truly a watershed year, the General Assembly transferred most state historic site projects from the Department of Conservation and Development and various commissions to the Department of Archives and History. The impetus for the legislation was a lengthy study conducted by the Institute of Government which concluded that moving historic site projects to the Department of Archives and History would centralize the state's historical activity. Properties conveyed immediately included Tryon Palace, the Zebulon B. Vance Birthplace, the Charles B. Aycock Birthplace, Town Creek Indian Mound, Alamance Battleground, the James Iredell House, and Brunswick Town. Conservation and Development retained responsibility for two historic properties—Fort Macon and Somerset Place—because of their status as state parks. Special appropriations in 1955 allowed for the purchase of the House in the Horseshoe and for plans to purchase land needed to develop Bentonville Battleground. Money was made available to enable the department to assist with four selected local restoration projects—the Barker House in Edenton, Gov. David Stone's Hope plantation house near Windsor, the Bunker Hill covered bridge near Claremont, and Historic Halifax. Additional legislation made it possible for the department to foster historic preservation projects being undertaken by other government agencies and private organizations.

To administer the state's initiatives in the realm of historic sites, the department established, effective October 1, 1955, the Division of Historic Sites and placed it under the supervision of William S. Tarlton. Initially only Town Creek Indian Mound and Alamance Battleground were managed directly by the new division. The James Iredell House and the House in the Horseshoe were supervised by Historic Sites but were operated by local nonprofit organizations. The remaining sites were still evolving.

The activities of the Division of Historic Sites were somewhat restricted, inasmuch as the agency's personnel and financial resources were limited. It was a time of exploration, both literally and figuratively, as the division learned about historic preservation in general, specific historic properties, and the bureaucracy that surrounded both. Even established sites such as Town Creek Indian Mound, which had been operating for seventeen years as an archaeological research site, needed museum facilities and restoration work. Of the division's initial biennium, it could be said that many plans were made but little progress was realized. Historic Halifax saw capital improvements in 1955 and 1956, with the state making a grant in the amount of $3,000 to the Historic Halifax Restoration Association, a local support group, which in turn purchased the town's Old Gaol, refurbished it, and established a museum within it. Similarly, the Barker House Association in Edenton received a grant in the amount of $1,200 to restore the historic Barker House. The House in the Horseshoe and the James Iredell House were the beneficiaries of local support of a different sort. Both properties were being restored and administered by local organizations under the supervision of the Department of Archives and History—the former by the Moore County Historical Association and the latter by the James Iredell House Association. The 1955 General Assembly created the Caswell Memorial Commission and appropriated $25,000 for the group to purchase, restore, and develop the site of Gov. Richard Caswell's presumed burial. The commission purchased the plot and surrounding acreage and donated the land to the state in 1956. Because of disagreements about the proposed nature of the memorial, no additional improvements were made to the site during the 1950s.

The Aycock Birthplace Historic Site on the day of its dedication, November 1, 1959.

In 1957 the state acquired fifty-one acres of the 6,000-acre battlefield at Bentonville. The property included the historic Harper House, which had been used as a hospital for Federal troops during the engagement; an adjoining Confederate cemetery; and various lines of earthworks. Completion of site development was targeted for 1965—in time for the centennial of the Battle of Bentonville.

Descendants of Charles B. Aycock donated to the state more than an acre of land and the house in which the governor was born in Wayne County. The state purchased eight additional acres and three original outbuildings, all of which were moved to the state-owned site. The buildings were restored to the period of Aycock's childhood and dedicated November 1, 1959, the centennial of his birth.

In 1952 Lawrence Lee, who since the early 1940s had led the crusade to save the remnants of the colonial-era settlement at Brunswick Town, supervised the archaeological survey of the site. Adequate remains were found—enough to merit preservation. Once an important port in the colony, Brunswick Town stood on property owned by the Sprunt family, which donated more than 114 acres to the state. The Episcopal Diocese of East Carolina donated an additional five acres, as well as the remaining walls of St. Philip's Church. Plans to develop the site were put on hold when military authorities at Sunny Point Army Terminal, an adjacent U.S. Army ammunition depot, objected to full-scale restoration for reasons of public safety. In 1957 the state and the federal government agreed to a restrictive easement under which the base commander at Sunny Point would have to approve any changes to the landscape at Brunswick Town. Reconstructed buildings were not planned for the colonial settlement; rather, Brunswick Town was intended to

be a site of strictly archaeological interest. In 1958 the Department of Archives and History employed Lee to complete thorough surveys of Brunswick Town and Fort Anderson, a nearby Civil War-era earthen fort. Excavation began at Brunswick Town that summer under staff archaeologist Stanley South, who continued to work at the site for ten years.

The ruins of the 1754 St. Philip's Anglican Church at Brunswick Town, pictured here, were investigated by archaeologists in the 1950s.

The agency received a tremendous boost on March 1, 1955, when a reclassification of personnel became effective. The action elevated professional standards by requiring a four-year college degree with a major in history or other social studies field for professional-level jobs and raised salaries substantially. The 1955 legislature also provided for merit-pay and cost-of-living increases. The combined pay increases and educational requirements boosted morale and made the agency more competitive in attracting applicants nationwide. While the department made unsuccessful attempts to secure a new building during the 1950s, staff members were fortunate in gaining much-needed space in a 1951 addition to the Education Building. Archives and History was assigned all of the first floor and half of the ground floor. The additional space permitted the expansion of services to the public and allowed for more efficient operation.

The Hall of History, or the state historical museum, as it was being called unofficially by then, expanded outreach programs in the 1950s. Efforts began with a Mobile Museum of History, which essentially involved filling a tractor-trailer that had been donated to the state in 1949 with historical artifacts and driving it throughout the state. From January 1950 to July 1951 the Mobile Museum toured the state with an exhibit of gifts of appreciation from the people of France

A 1950 photograph of the staff of the Department of Archives and History. *Left to right, front row,* Manora Mewborn, Julia C. Meconnahey, Blanche M. Johnson, Eloise Sarvis, and May Davis Hill. *Second row,* William S. Powell, Frances Harmon Whitley, Mary J. Rogers, Eva J. Lawrence, Gwyn Woodard, and Dorothy Reynolds. *Third row,* W. F. Burton, Christopher Crittenden, Charles Jones, Edward Freeman, Marvin Rogers, and D. L. Corbitt. Joye Jordan was the only member of the staff not included in the photograph.

The Mobile Museum of History, which began operation in 1950, continued to travel the state through the Carolina Charter Tercentenary in 1963 and into the early 1970s.

for the efforts expended by North Carolinians during World War II. Although more people were able to enjoy the exhibit in the Mobile Museum than at the Hall of History in Raleigh, the program was eventually discontinued because of a lack of funding. In 1953 the Hall of History launched a program for young people called the Tar Heel Junior Historian Association; the first clubs, formed in association with schools, were organized the following year. In 1959 the Hall of History hired Sue Ridge, a curator within the education program, to manage the Junior Historian program. Ridge began sending out mailings to school principals, asking for the names of teachers who might be interested in serving as club advisers. She then contacted those teachers and invited them to a workshop, at which they were offered speakers, activities, and a museum tour. During the 1956-1958 biennium the Hall of History prepared educational slide programs with scripts and made them available to teachers and other interested organizations throughout the state. Topics included Cherokee Indians, the Lost Colony, mysteries and legends, Wedgwood pottery, and early architecture. The slide loan program was so popular that within two years the twelve presentations were booked every week of the school year. The present incarnation of the program features at least five copies of each of forty-one available titles. Teacher-resource materials accompany many titles. Exhibition-related notebooks, curriculum-related lesson plans, and reproduction artifacts are included with other slide programs. More than 100,000 people see the programs each year.

In 1951 the legislature decreed that microfilm copies of records would have the same legal standing as original paper records. Statutory and judicial recognition of the format gave the State Archives the option to microfilm state agency records and destroy the originals, a critical move in the progression toward implementing modern records management. In order to store the mounting semicurrent records and to house the growing microfilm unit, the department needed a proper records center. Construction of such a building commenced in

The North Carolina Newspaper Project: Preserving the Printed Word

With many of North Carolina's newspapers in danger of being lost, Archives and History in the 1950s began identifying and microfilming newspapers. Over the succeeding four decades, the North Carolina Newspaper Project (initially known as the Newspaper Microfilm Project) permanently preserved on microfilm hundreds of titles and millions of newspaper pages. The 1958-1959 biennial report noted that "probably no program undertaken by the Department will be of more significance to historians throughout the country."

In 1959 legislators approved approximately $28,000 to microfilm state newspapers published before 1870; that initial effort in time expanded to include later-nineteenth- and, eventually, twentieth-century papers. When original papers could be found in North Carolina, they were borrowed and brought to Raleigh to be filmed. If no satisfactory copy was available in state, the staff obtained a copy from out-of-state sources. The first newspaper filmed was the *Raleigh Register,* its run extending from 1799 to 1886. By mid-1962 a total of 543 reels had been made available for public use. In that year Archives and History issued the first edition of *North Carolina Newspapers on Microfilm.* Six editions of that guide were published between 1962 and 1984. In 1963 the department and the North Carolina Library Association produced the more complete *Union List of North Carolina Newspapers, 1751-1900.*

Between 1959 and 1972 the Newspaper Project created approximately 2,400 reels of film. By June 1974 the staff had turned to the systematic approach of finding newspapers county-by-county instead of randomly selecting titles; however, during the 1970s and 1980s the number of reels completed declined. Staffing and equipment problems contributed to the slowdown, and by the 1982-1984 biennium only twenty-three reels were produced. By the end of the decade, however, there was renewed interest in the project. Production increased, as did entries into a database that cataloged each issue held on microfilm.

Increased attention to identifying, cataloging, and filming extant North Carolina newspapers reached a peak in the 1990s. North Carolina joined states from throughout the nation as part of the United States Newspaper Program. With funding from the National Endowment for the Humanities totaling more than $1.3 million, the Division (former Department) of Archives and History in collaboration with the State Library of North Carolina completed a county-by-county field survey to identify newspapers in libraries, archives, newspaper offices, and in private ownership. Newspapers, including previously unknown titles, were located and cataloged. With the assistance of grant-funded staff, existing Archives and History film holdings were inventoried and inspected; deteriorating master reels were duplicated; selected titles from each county, including rare African American and foreign-language newspapers, were microfilmed; and a revised *Guide to North Carolina Newspapers on Microfilm* was made available on the Internet. During the 1990s more than three million pages were added to agency holdings.—*Dennis F. Daniels*

As part of the North Carolina Newspaper Project, staff members microfilmed known copies of North Carolina newspapers published from 1751 to 1900. Pictured here, (*left to right*): H. G. Jones, State Archivist; Thomas Britt; Michael Machesko; and Cecil Miller. Britt headed the project from 1959 to 1968.

The Tar Heel Junior Historian Association: Museum Outreach to Students

The Tar Heel Junior Historian Association (THJHA), which observes its fiftieth anniversary in 2003, has taken the lead in furthering the study of state history in the public schools. In recent years the organization, based in the North Carolina Museum of History (NCMOH), has averaged about eight thousand members, principally students in grades four through eight. In the early 1950s William H. Cartwright, chairman of Duke University's Department of Education, and educator J. C. McLendon worked to create such a program. They studied junior history programs in other states and met with Christopher Crittenden and Charles F. Carroll, state superintendent of public instruction. In April 1953 legislators endorsed the concept, and the Hall of History, then led by Joye Jordan, gave the program life. In 1954, the first full year, three clubs were formed; by 1956 forty had been created. The 1956-1958 report of the THJHA noted the need for a full-time staff member. By 1958 the number of clubs had dropped to twenty-nine. Lack of attention was cited as the reason most clubs failed.

During the 1961-1962 school year, the association first issued the *Tar Heel Junior Historian* magazine (publication of which continues to the present). In 1962 the THJHA held its first project competition; in subsequent years the North Carolina Literary and Historical Association sponsored awards for winners. By 1965-1966 the number of students enrolled in clubs had risen to 3,379. In the 1971 academic year public schools removed North Carolina history from the curriculum and, as a consequence, THJHA membership declined. The following year a combined two-year course in United States and North Carolina history for eighth- and ninth-graders was added, and by 1974 the numbers were back up. The North Carolina History Quiz (later renamed the Christopher Crittenden State History Quiz) was inaugurated in 1976.

By 1980 the association had 4,808 members, the highest enrollment up to that time. The increase was attributed to the employment of a field representative. The NCMOH support organization, the Museum of History Associates, sent subscriptions to the *Tar Heel Junior Historian* magazine to all public and school libraries in the state. In 1982 the association

---

1952 and was completed the following year. The facility, located at the corner of Lane and McDowell Streets, is presently known as the "Old Records Center." Its supervisor was responsible for seeing that records disposition schedules were observed. Such schedules, as prepared by the department's archivists, were designed to address a lack of storage space at the agencies, as well as at the records center; to make the microfilming process more economical; and to preserve only the most valuable records. The notable success of the records management program garnered the support of the Council of State and caught the attention of the state agencies, as well as county and municipal governments. Those entities called upon State Archives staffers to analyze various records and assist in the creation of records management systems. An appropriations bill was passed in 1959 to fund the local records program. In a further effort to preserve records of a historical nature, the General Assembly appropriated approximately $28,000 in 1959 to microfilm all state newspapers before 1870.

In the fifties the Department of Archives and History at that time served Tryon Palace in an administrative and advisory capacity. The agency handled accounting and budgetary matters while providing advice on historical and

presented its first Afro-American History Award. The reintroduction of North Carolina history as a separate eighth-grade course in 1983 increased enrollment numbers to 10,651. In the 1982-1984 biennium the THJHA and the North Carolina Coordinating Committee for the Advancement of History obtained a grant to make a slide/tape production on selected North Carolina history topics. In the fall of 1986 the THJHA supplemented the magazine with its *Crossroads* newsletter.

A group of eighth-grade students viewing a street scene exhibit in the Hall of History. During the 1958 to 1960 biennium, over 75,000 students visited the Hall of History.

In the 1990s the NCMOH and the association expanded the material available to students on the Internet. An essay contest was introduced in 1993. In 1995 the THJHA Gallery opened in the new NCMOH building. During the 1994-1996 period the association created a video (funded by a grant) and distributed it to public schools. In that biennium the THJHA introduced the *Adviser Newsletter* and initiated workshops for members in conjunction with Catawba College and Aycock Birthplace; in succeeding years workshops were held at the North Carolina Transportation Museum, Tryon Palace, and the Mountain Gateway Museum. Enrollment figures by 2000 stood at 8,269.— *Dennis F. Daniels*

operational questions. The Tryon Palace Commission maintained a primary focus on completing the restoration while seeking out and purchasing appropriate furnishings. In 1956 Gertrude Carraway stepped down from the Palace Commission in order to become head of the newly designated Tryon Palace Restoration Complex. In that capacity she directed the grand opening of the palace on April 10, 1959. Two days prior to the public opening, both houses of the General Assembly met in the building's restored legislative chambers for a ceremonial session. That year all of the properties and furnishings associated with the complex were deeded to the state; admission fees (two dollars for adults and one dollar for children) were deposited with the state treasurer. The Tryon Palace Restoration Complex operated as its own section within the department at that time and functions as a semi-autonomous part of the agency to this day.

In May 1952 the Department of Archives and History began publishing a bimonthly newsletter called *Carolina Comments*. Designed to highlight departmental activities, the newsletter augmented the "Historical News" section of the *North Carolina Historical Review. Carolina Comments*, prepared by the director's office at the time, was distributed to members of the state's Literary and Historical Association, subscribers to the *North Carolina Historical Review*, and public

Ted R. Edwards selling pamphlets prepared by the Department of Archives and History. The student on the right is holding a copy of *The Pirates of Colonial North Carolina*, first published in 1960. The most popular title ever published by the Historical Publications Section, the pamphlet has never gone out of print and, as of 2001, was in its twenty-first printing.

libraries throughout the state. In 1956 the Historical Publications Section implemented an across-the-board increase in the price of its publications. Subscriptions to the *North Carolina Historical Review* went from $2 to $3 per year—the first such increase in the price of the journal. Documentary and case-bound volumes increased from $1 to $3 each. All charts, pamphlets, and leaflets were assigned a nominal fee (they had previously been sent free of charge to libraries, teachers, and subscribers to the *Review*.) A kit including some of these educational materials was assembled and made available at a cost of $1. All of these charges were made necessary because of increases in printing and paper costs. At the same time, sales increased by 41 percent over the previous biennium, so the costs were not deemed prohibitive, as they had been in the 1930s.

The General Assembly of 1959 established two bodies that would play noteworthy roles—the Carolina Charter Tercentenary Commission and the North Carolina Confederate Centennial Commission. The legislature directed the Charter Commission to plan a program to celebrate the three hundredth anniversary of King Charles II's granting of the Carolina Charter in 1663. The commission's most lasting contribution was the creation and early administration of the Colonial Records Project, an ambitious program to publish a series of documents relevant to the colonial history of North Carolina; the project was transferred to the Historical Publications Section in 1964 upon the dissolution of the Charter Commission. The other important organization established in 1959 was the North Carolina Confederate Centennial Commission. That body, an active and productive association, initiated significant publications, including the series *North Carolina Troops, 1861-1865: A Roster*. The Confederate Centennial Commission was also instrumental in planning programs and commemorations of the Civil War, arranging the salvage of sunken vessels, and even orchestrating the return to North Carolina of Gov. Zebulon Vance's captured wartime letter books held by the National Archives. Once the commission had completed its charge in 1965, the roster project was first transferred to the Archives and Records Section and then, in 1974, to the Historical Publications Section, where it remains.

7

The Sixties: A Modern Home for the Agency

In 1959, when the Department of Archives and History occupied 40,000 square feet in the Education Building, its actual space needs were estimated at 130,000 square feet. Of course, the Education Building was only the agency's primary headquarters; by that time the department operated out of four other locations in Raleigh. The Department of Archives and History required a specially constructed facility in order to meet the demands of its mission. With circumstances as they were in 1961, the department lacked storage, work, and office space; experienced adverse temperature conditions in records storage areas; had an insufficient Search Room for the increasing numbers of patrons; needed public rest rooms for visitors to the Hall of History; and experienced dampness and mildew from exposed heating pipes in the ceiling of records storage areas, a situation that could result in tremendous damage in the event of leaks. Much publicity was circulated about these and other deficits and about the various other southern states that had freestanding archives or state library buildings. In a seemingly desperate attempt to appeal to the General Assembly and other influential parties

involved with the recently appointed commissions, a proposal was made to name a new Archives and History facility the "Carolina Charter and Confederate Memorial Building." Fortunately for all involved, that idea was dropped by the time the building became a reality.

In an effort to convey the need for a new facility, State Archivist H. G. Jones showed Governor Terry Sanford the exposed steam pipes in the Archives stacks of the Education Building.

The Archives and History/State Library Building (west end) under construction in 1967 (*above*). The 155,000 square foot facility was dedicated on May 15, 1969. A few months before his death in October 1969, Dr. Christopher Crittenden proudly posed behind the recently completed structure (*below*).

The appropriation for the building came in 1963—but not without compromise. Rather than getting its own building of 131,000 square feet, the Department of Archives and History gained a structure to house portions of its operations, as well as those of the State Library, with a total of 155,000 square feet for the two agencies. Space in the new building was about 40 percent less than either agency had requested. Fortunately, the new building would still be constructed to include an underground security vault and a deep-tank microfilm processor. At the time it was believed that the State Library would move into its own building within a few years, as soon as an appropriation was made to that effect, and that its space would revert to Archives and History. Other ambitious plans for the building called for murals and sculptures in the front lobby. However, because of budgetary contraints the plans were abandoned. A few days before the May 15, 1969, dedication of the new Archives and History/State Library Building, a newspaper reporter wrote: "Like women's skirts, the building is eye-catching, expensive and entirely too small to serve its purpose effectively."

In planning for the new building, administrators envisioned murals and sculptures for the front lobby. Adolfo Delgado, a Mexican artist, submitted a proposed mural depicting scenes from North Carolina history. Budgetary constraints forced the plans to be scrapped. A portion of the artwork is pictured here.

Meanwhile, in the early 1960s, reconstruction of the homestead at Bennett Place was just getting under way. Frank Kenan, a prominent North Carolina businessman and philanthropist, discovered on the nearby Proctor family property a condemned house that was subsequently determined to be the approximate age and size of the original Bennett dwelling. The house was moved to the site and restored, with only the separate kitchen requiring reconstruction. The structures were dedicated in 1962. In 1960 reconstruction began on the Zebulon B. Vance Birthplace in Buncombe County. Hewn yellow pine logs were used to build on the original foundation around the original chimney. Four outbuildings—a loom house, a springhouse, a toolhouse, and slave quarters—were constructed on the property, and the site was dedicated May 13, 1961—the anniversary of Vance's birth. In 1968 Vance Birthplace held its first Pioneer Living Days, with demonstrations of historical daily household activities. The popular event, now held semiannually, is the oldest ongoing special event within the state Historic Sites system. Also in 1960, Archives and History began developing a historic site at Fort Fisher. The remains of the fort became a National Historic Landmark in 1961. New Hanover County transferred Battle Acre, a half-acre tract encompassing a United Daughters of the Confederacy monument, to the state; a small

Pioneer Living Days, here featuring a demonstration of woodworking techniques, has been a popular event at the Vance Birthplace since its inception in 1968.

museum pavilion was constructed there. The new facility, dedicated and opened in 1962, proved inadequate to serve the large crowds that visited the site. A full visitor center was opened in 1965. Boosting attendance at the fort was the recovery of the *Modern Greece*, a Civil War blockade-runner, a project begun in 1962. Salvage of the vessel ultimately led to the establishment of the Department of Archives and History's Underwater Archaeology Unit in 1967 and the department's preservation lab at Fort Fisher. The lab was built cooperatively with the U.S. Navy and the North Carolina Confederate Centennial Commission.

The Alamance Battleground visitor center was completed in 1960, and the site was dedicated on May 16, 1961. The following year, the Regulator Column, erected at Guilford Battleground National Military Park in 1901, was moved to Alamance Battleground, albeit not without a good deal of controversy. In 1966 the John Allen House, an authentic frontier structure contemporary with the Regulator movement, was moved to Alamance Battleground to enhance interpretation at the site. Also in 1961, Archives and History established the Bentonville Battleground Advisory Committee, which superseded the 1957 citizen's association that had purchased the initial fifty-one acres, including the Harper House. Funding was secured for a visitor center, which was dedicated on March 21, 1965, the centennial of the battle's final day. In November 1961 the Oak Plain School, a nearby one-room schoolhouse thought to be contemporary with the childhood of Gov. Charles B. Aycock, was moved to the Aycock Birthplace site. (In the late 1980s it was determined that the school was actually built in 1893; the structure was restored appropriately and the interpretation was altered to that of a school contemporary to Aycock's governorship.) In 1961 the legislature appropriated money for a visitor center, which opened the following year. Also in 1961 at Town Creek Indian Mound, another of the state's most popular sites, the Native American mortuary was reconstructed and twenty-eight burials were excavated and prepared for exhibit. A visitor center was dedicated at that site in April 1963. That same year the General Assembly designated Bath as a state historic site in a cooperative venture with the Historic

The North Carolina Confederate Centennial Commission, July 1960–June 1965

On the eve of the centennial of the American Civil War, the federal government prepared to commemorate the nation's most tragic and defining event. In honoring both sides without fanning the flames of "bitterness and hatred engendered by the conflict a century ago," the United States Civil War Centennial Commission sought to foster "a new study of American patriotism." Following the actions of Virginia and other states, North Carolina established its own commission to represent the Tar Heel State in the celebration. The North Carolina Confederate Centennial Commission assembled an ambitious agenda, placing emphasis on research and publication. The state, home to a number of prominent war-related sites, held untapped potential for increased tourism. A nonprofit corporation was formed to raise money, and county subcommittees planned local events throughout the state. The General Assembly appropriated additional funds for commemorative efforts and passed a resolution restricting use of the Confederate flag to "dignified occasions."

Working closely with the Department of Archives and History, the commission launched or assisted with a number of landmark endeavors that to this day promote research and tourism in North Carolina. These projects included: development of historic sites; salvage work at underwater archaeological sites; erection of highway historical markers for all of the state's notable Civil War locations; and publication of a multivolume roster of North Carolina's Civil War soldiers (the latter an exhaustive and highly acclaimed series still in the process of completion). Extending the commission's educational reach, the North Carolina Museum of History's "Mobile Museum of History" toured the state with updated exhibits highlighting North Carolina's wartime experiences. In 1965, capping off four years of research and development, commemorative events were held at Fort Fisher, Bentonville Battleground, and Bennett Place State Historic Sites—each marking pivotal events in the final months of the war in North Carolina. In April of that year Vice-President Hubert H. Humphrey spoke at a "Centennial of National Unity" program at Bennett Place, site of the war's largest troop surrender. The event was covered on national television, a highlight of the state commission's tenure.

As the nationwide observance drew to a close, the national commission awarded North Carolina the Bronze Medallion, which recognized meritorious participation. In a presentation in Raleigh by director James I. Robertson, the Tar Heel State became the first in the nation to receive the recognition. The University of North Carolina Press received a separate medallion for excellence in publishing, making North Carolina the only state with two recipients of the honor. The medal was inscribed with the phrases "Let us have peace" and "consciousness of duty faithfully performed."

As the state commission disbanded, executive secretary Norman Larson appealed for a lasting remembrance: "Let us hope that with the end of the centennial our interest in this most exciting era in American history will not waver. Rather, let us use the centennial as a foundation on which to build a greater appreciation and understanding so that future generations will have complete and total knowledge of the American Civil War." Four decades removed from that foundation, the state's war-related sites and exhibits are among the most studied and visited historical attractions in North Carolina.—*Mark Anderson Moore*

Bath Commission, with the commission to assist in acquiring and furnishing properties. Between 1964 and 1965 the Historic Bath Commission transferred ownership of all its historic properties to the state.

In May 1963, as part of the Civil War Centennial, D. C. Murray, a house mover from Rose Hill who was hired by the Kinston City Council and the

Lenoir County Commissioners, successfully raised from the bottom of the Neuse River the Civil War gunboat CSS *Neuse*. For a year the ironclad vessel was exposed to the elements and to vandals. Archives and History received permission from the Caswell Memorial Commission to relocate the boat to the memorial park. Gov. Terry Sanford authorized the use of ten thousand dollars in emergency funds to move the vessel and treat it with a preservative. The relocation was accomplished in May 1964 by cutting the hull into three pieces and moving them separately, rejoining them at the site. At that point the site became known as the Caswell-*Neuse* State Historic Site. After seven years of negotiations and planning, the James K. Polk Birthplace became a state historic site in 1964. The foundation for the original house was not located by archaeologists; it was determined that U.S. Highway 521 likely passed over it. In 1966 four log structures were donated to the state for use in the reconstruction of the Polk farmhouse and outbuildings. Contemporaneous interior paneling for the buildings was secured from a house under demolition in Moore County. Also during 1966 Historic Sites staff members were involved in a court case about the purported "Daniel Boone homeplace." The plaintiff wanted a marker erected at the spot, but there was not enough corroborating evidence to do so.

The Confederate ram *Neuse* being raised from the Neuse River in the fall of 1961. The ironclad was burned by its crew to prevent its capture when Union troops occupied Kinston in March 1865. The raising of the boat was one of many Civil War-related projects in which the Department of Archives and History participated during the Civil War centennial.

Following several years of Archives and History involvement and support, Historic Halifax was established as a state historic site in 1965. Over the next four years the Historic Halifax Restoration Association transferred about twenty-five acres of land to the state. In 1969 Historic Halifax became the state's first district nomination to the National Register of Historic Places. Likewise garnering state attention in the late 1960s was Fort Dobbs, near Statesville, at which archaeological excavations were conducted. The excavations uncovered part of the fort's foundations. Research conducted by Jerry C. Cashion, then a graduate student in history at the University of North Carolina at Chapel Hill, failed to turn up a full description of the fort, however, and the decision was made not to attempt to

"In the Matter of Daniel Boone"

The scene was extraordinary. On April 25, 1966, in the old Education Building, then home to the Department of Archives and History (A&H), attorneys took center stage in a public hearing titled "In the Matter of the Daniel Boone Association, Inc., Petitioners, vs. the Historic Sites Advisory Committee, Respondents." At issue was the authenticity of the purported "Daniel Boone homeplace" in Davidson County.

It was not the first time that Boone had been the focus of public attention. In 1919 the North Carolina Historical Commission cosponsored a plaque indicating that young Boone had settled alongside the Yadkin River with his father, Squire Boone. J. Hampton Rich (1874-1949), Davie County native and sometime newspaper editor, devoted his life to promoting the Boone name and legend. At sites throughout the nation, including sixty-six in North Carolina from Bryson City to Clinton, the flamboyant Rich erected monuments, many featuring a large arrowhead. Most displayed a likeness of the frontiersman sitting on a boulder with his dog, his rifle, and his powder horn at his side. One made

This familiar image of Daniel Boone was emblazoned on numerous markers erected by J. Hampton Rich.

its way briefly onto the State Capitol grounds in 1943 before being removed. "Fact is if Dan had gone to all the places where Hamp has put monuments to mark his passing, he would have been the travelingest pioneer known to history, sacred or profane," editorialized the *Raleigh Times*.

Wade Sowers, a dentist who placed family tradition at the center of his case, led the effort to authenticate the Davidson County site, on which a cabin had been reconstructed near local landmarks known as Boone's Cave and Boone's Ford. In 1963 the legislature appropriated fifteen thousand dollars for purchase of the property subject to review by A&H. After conducting an extensive study, A&H staff concluded that the site could not be authenticated. They pointed out that additional claims had associated Boone with numerous sites in the Piedmont, all without basis.

The persistence of the plaintiffs was remarkable. In November 1965 a Wake County Superior Court judge reviewed their appeal and remanded the case to A&H; the aforementioned April 1966 hearing was the consequence. Attorneys for the petitioners cited the 1919 plaque as precedent, but Christopher Crittenden, director of A&H, pointed out that the text of the plaque did not specify a site. The plaintiffs cited secondary studies, as well as manuscripts collected by Wisconsin archivist Lyman Draper, as evidence in support of their contentions. Much discussion revolved around a stone (since lost) inscribed with Boone's name. Newspapers had a field day with the ruckus.

In each case, A&H staff countered that contemporary primary source evidence was insufficient to fix a site. The staff pointed out that Boone was a squatter and left scarcely any record of his life in North Carolina. In April 1967 another superior court judge reviewed the case and tossed it back to A&H. (The petitioners elected not to appeal to the state supreme court.) A&H erected a highway historical marker in Davie County upon the 640-acre "Boone Tract" acquired in 1752 by Squire Boone. Boone's Cave was made a part of the state parks system but in 2002 was transferred to Davidson County for development as a local park.—*Michael Hill*

reconstruct the fortification. In 1969 a legislative appropriation requiring matching funds established Fort Dobbs as a state historic site and passive recreational park. With help from the Smith Richardson Foundation of Greensboro, the Iredell County Historical Society raised funds to acquire land and develop a site at Fort Dobbs, the only remaining vestige of North Carolina's participation in the French and Indian War. In 1969 the buildings at Somerset plantation and the land surrounding them were designated a state historic site, and Archives and History assumed responsibility (previously held by the Department of Conservation and Development, Division of State Parks) for maintaining the new facility. The present-day historic site, known as Somerset Place, includes 31 of the original lakeside acres, 7 original nineteenth-century buildings, 2 reconstructed slave quarters (large and small), and a reconstructed slave hospital.

As the Division of Historic Sites matured, attempts were made to standardize job descriptions and operating procedures at the respective sites. During the 1964-1966 biennium, the division consolidated individual site budgets and established a centralized supply warehouse in order to streamline operations. In an attempt to consolidate staff and responsibilities, the museums and historic sites divisions merged in November 1969 to become the Division of Historic Sites and Museums; Joye Jordan, formerly head of the Division of Museums, assumed charge of the new entity. The combination of the two agencies lasted only until 1974, however.

For the Hall of History, the early 1960s were a time to revitalize Civil War artifacts and exhibits in preparation for and celebration of the centennial of that event. The museum expanded public outreach through five new traveling exhibits—four of which were related to the Civil War—and through the new periodical *Tar Heel Junior Historian*, introduced in 1962. The Mobile Museum was reintroduced in 1963, when Chevrolet/General Motors donated a tractor-trailer and R. J. Reynolds Tobacco Company provided $35,000 for operating costs. The first series of mobile exhibits focused on the colonial period in conjunction with the Carolina Charter Tercentenary.

In preparation for the move to the new building, the Hall of History in July 1965 became the North Carolina Museum of History, a name that better represented the full extent of the section's mission and scope. In readying for the move, the museum updated all of its accession records and improved finding aids in the staff's research library. For two years prior to the move, the museum laboratory was busy cleaning collections such as its oil portraits of famous North Carolinians and its militaria; it cleaned and preserved leather goods and fumigated all its collections. At about that same time, the employees of the laboratory at Fort Fisher were working to preserve recovered artifacts, primarily those from the CSS *Neuse*. In October 1969 the museum initiated a more structured docent-training program. It developed a training notebook and required docents to

The Carolina Charter Tercentenary Commission: Commemorating the Three Hundredth Birthday

In 1948 former governor J. Melville Broughton invited contributions for a most unusual cause. "A short time ago," he wrote, there had "turned up in England a document which, upon careful investigation, has proved to be the original Charter of Carolina." This was nothing less than North Carolina's birth certificate, and state officials lost no time in authenticating and acquiring the rare gem from the British dealer. Private money covered the cost of the document (just over six thousand dollars), and the Carolina Charter soon found its way to Raleigh. In 1959 the General Assembly established a commission to plan and conduct a celebration honoring the three hundredth anniversary of the Charter, which had been granted by England's King Charles II to eight Lords Proprietors in 1663. It was under those loyal supporters of Charles II—in the wake of previous failed efforts in the region—that permanent colonization of Carolina began. Beyond the Charter, the scope of the celebration was extended to include the first century of official existence of the colony—that is, to 1763. That extension allowed for a more geographically diverse, statewide celebration.

The authorizing legislation called for the appointment of twenty-two commission members plus three ex officio panelists—the director of the Department of Archives and History, the superintendent of public instruction, and the director of the North Carolina Department of Conservation and Development. Commissioner Chalmers Davidson noted that North Carolina's three hundredth year marked "an appropriate milestone at which to take note of where we are and how we got here." The commission sponsored commemorative events throughout the state, promoting activities to highlight North Carolina's colonial history. Those efforts included production of a musical drama for television, a commemorative work for a symphony orchestra, an educational film for students, and an exhibit featuring rare artworks from England. Numerous historical publications were produced, many designed for use in public schools. The publication initiative included the commission's landmark endeavor to revive the *Colonial Records of North Carolina* series (an enterprise that continues to this day). The commission ceased to function on December 31, 1963, the last day of the tercentennial year, but its influence continued. The group had endorsed long-standing plans for a building that could house the Charter and other "priceless archives," while at the same time accommodating a "modern, efficient historical museum." That building was completed in 1968.

Formed as an auxiliary nonprofit organization in 1960 was the Carolina Charter Corporation. That group's purpose was to support the celebration and to solicit donations for related undertakings. The corporation continues to meet annually. Presently its primary role is to support the gathering and publication of North Carolina's colonial records. From its inception the corporation has provided much of the funding for the research into and the copying of early North Carolina documents in English, Scottish, and Irish archives. Major funding sources for its work include the North Carolina Society of the Cincinnati, the Z. Smith Reynolds Foundation, the National Endowment for the Humanities, the Kellenberger Historical Foundation, and other interested organizations and individuals.—*Mark Anderson Moore*

attend twelve hours of classroom instruction and to complete a series of required readings before assuming their volunteer duties. Staff development received a boost in November 1969 when two members of the museum's education staff visited a ninety-one-year-old North Carolina woman who taught them the craft of spinning. They, in turn, taught other staffers and docents, so that traditional

Approximately one-half of the 132 staff members of the Department of Archives and History on the steps of the Education Building in 1966.

spinning could be demonstrated to museum visitors. Weaving and pottery demonstrations were subsequently added.

For the State Archives staff, public demand and statutory changes in the 1960s mandated the updating of programs and services. The Search Room began opening on Saturdays from 8:30 A.M. to 1:30 P.M. on a trial basis in November 1963. There had been complaints both to the State Archives and to the Governor's Office that the Search Room did not maintain operating hours convenient to citizens who worked Mondays through Fridays. In response, the staff began opening on Saturdays as an experiment, with the understanding that if the opening was not embraced by the public, it would be discontinued. Of course, Saturday became the busiest day of the week and has remained so ever since. Once all of the State Archives' holdings were moved to the new building in February 1969 (a process requiring two weeks), the number of researchers visiting the agency increased by 40 percent.

In 1960 what was then known as the State Records Section distributed the *County Records Manual*, believed to be the first of its kind in the nation; the manual offered information on scheduling records for retention or disposal. It was unprecedented in records management, and agencies in twenty-two other states and three foreign countries requested copies for study. The following year Archives and History prepared and distributed a similar handbook for municipalities. In 1961 the General Assembly enacted legislation that expanded the responsibilities and staff size of the State Records Section. Chapter 132 of the General Statutes gave Archives and History responsibility for administering a program for the "application of efficient & economical management methods to the creation, utilization, maintenance, retention, preservation, and disposal of official records. . . ." The section was likewise charged with establishing standards and procedures for managing public records at the state and local level. On January 24, 1962, Gov. Terry Sanford issued a directive calling the attention of all state agencies to the records management program and requesting them to complete records schedules within five months. In October 1964 the Society of American Archivists honored North Carolina's archival records management program by presenting to the Division of Archives and Manuscripts the society's first distinguished service award for "outstanding services to the American people and for exemplary contributions to the archival profession."

By the end of the 1950s, the State Archives was completing approximately six thousand reels of microfilm per year, all of which were processed commercially. In July 1961 the department established its own Microfilm Services Center, including a processing laboratory, in the basement of the Old YMCA Building at the corner of Wilmington and Edenton Streets. The initial equipment cost about twenty thousand dollars. With the burden of processing film for the Newspaper Project, an ambitious program to microfilm every North Carolina newspaper ever in print, the center was inadequately staffed to perform the work generated. However, through receipts and budgetary juggling, two more positions were created by 1962. By the middle of the decade, the Newspaper Project had slowed, altering the priorities in film processing. Soon all microfilm processing was handled in-house.

The comprehensive local records program established in 1959, which included microfilm operations, preparation of inventories and schedules, and document restoration, accelerated the collecting of county records, which had been an ongoing concern of the State Archives since the early efforts in the field by Fred Olds. Yet the lack of staff left many collections unarranged and unavailable. As a result of the museum's efforts to reorganize and catalog its holdings during the 1962-1964 biennium, all documents within museum collections were transferred to the State Archives—again increasing diversity. One noteworthy addition to the Archives' holdings were the Black Mountain College Records, accepted in 1963. The records had been in storage since the college closed in 1956. Once the papers were accessioned, the Archives registrar began serving as registrar for the college records as well, providing transcripts and other information for former students. The nonrestricted general records of Black Mountain College have been used continuously since their arrival in Raleigh by those interested in the institution's faculty and students and the college's enduring influence on art, literature, and higher education. Furthermore a mandate requires the State Archives to accept student records from defunct North Carolina colleges and technical schools that request the service.

For the Historical Publications Section, the 1960s were a time for expanding public presence and for developing new programs. The promotion of available materials was augmented through radio and television announcements, press releases, and cooperation with the State Library and the North Carolina Department

Architectural Surveys: A Lasting Record of the State's Historic Properties

Born of the preservation-friendly era following World War II, the state's architectural survey program identifies, documents, and promotes North Carolina's architectural heritage. For more than thirty years, what is now the Historic Preservation Office (HPO) has sponsored local and regional surveys. Collectively, the data constitutes one of the most comprehensive programs of its kind in the United States. Catherine W. Bishir, architectural historian and longtime coordinator of the survey program, addressed the distinctiveness of the state's built environment: "It is not so much the grandeur or fame of its individual landmarks that defines North Carolina's architectural heritage, but its intensely regional and local character, the sense of place, which captivates the traveler and sustains the residents in this old state."

As permanent records—with detailed reports, maps, and photos—the inventories provide the underpinning for a host of preservation actions. Survey data directly influences decisions regarding nominations to the National

By 2002, surveys of historic architecture had been completed for fifty-eight North Carolina counties and roughly sixty municipalities. Catherine Bishir, architectural historian and longtime coordinator of the survey program, is shown here at "Tusculum," a circa 1831 Warren County plantation home.

of Public Instruction. That publicity, coupled with an increased number of titles, increased the section's sales figures for the first biennium of the 1960s to more than triple those of the previous one. In two years the sales figures skyrocketed from 57,706 items to 187,998. With continued efforts, sales rose again in the ensuing biennium, to 444,919. Between 1962 and 1964 the section enhanced its image by issuing documentary volumes in dust jackets; the first such work was volume 1 of *The Papers of Zebulon Baird Vance*, issued in 1963.

Employing an effective direct marketing strategy, Historical Publications and the Hall of History jointly opened a sales desk in the spring of 1964, making the department's publications easily accessible to people visiting the museum and/or the State Archives. In the fall of 1964 Historical Publications, with the assistance of a committee including members of the Department of Public Instruction, created a North Carolina history kit and distributed it to supervisors of North Carolina history teachers in the public schools. Included in the kit were sample copies of departmental pamphlets and a current list of publications. The Department of Public Instruction began sending the Historical Publications catalog to

Register of Historic Places, the impact of government projects on historic properties, the efforts of local preservation groups, and private investment in historic structures. The records form the bedrock of preservation planning, providing the basis for future success in the field. Beginning in 1967, staff members—with assistance from local preservationists and historians—worked on several of the state's most prominent historic sites. In the late 1970s, with the aid of matching grants to county and local sponsors, more comprehensive assessments emerged. The program grew steadily, encompassing a full range of architecturally and historically significant properties. By 2002, surveys had been completed for fifty-eight of North Carolina's one hundred counties and for approximately sixty municipalities. Complementary thematic surveys cover specific subjects such as truss bridges, county courthouses, and twentieth-century suburbs.

A principal goal of the program has been the publication of architectural surveys. While local or private sponsors pay for the design and printing of such books, the content is usually compiled in projects cosponsored and supervised by the HPO. These works typically offer an illustrated overview with a catalog of individual properties and neighborhoods. To date, more than forty county surveys and more than thirty municipal surveys have been published. That valuable series, on a level unmatched by any other state, provides a popular and accessible portrait of individual communities and properties. A few of the published architectural surveys have received national awards for excellence. Broader studies have emerged from the program, including *A Guide to the Historic Architecture of Eastern North Carolina* (UNC Press, 1996). A sister volume for western North Carolina appeared in 1999, and a third volume covering the Piedmont region is currently in production.

North Carolina enjoys a proud record in the field of historic preservation. From the mountains to the coast, familiar sights have been re-illuminated. Citizens have been encouraged to restore old buildings and to rejuvenate traditional neighborhoods. In the new millennium, a strong state and local commitment to preservation in North Carolina continues to sustain the long-standing program—an endeavor that has fostered a lasting record of North Carolina's rich architectural heritage.—*Mark Anderson Moore*

school libraries in semiannual bulk mailings. This joint effort, and continued cooperation, has helped to get educational materials into the schools, thereby boosting sales and visibility.

As the Carolina Charter Tercentenary Commission and the North Carolina Confederate Centennial Commission terminated their activities in the mid–1960s, segments of the organizations were transferred to the Department of Archives and History. Materials previously published by the Tercentenary Commission were turned over to Historical Publications to distribute and sell. The Colonial Records Project was transferred to Historical Publications in 1969. In January 1967, responsibility for generating the then bimonthly departmental newsletter *Carolina Comments* was transferred from the director's office to Historical Publications. It was at that time that the newsletter's format was altered so that it would be the same size as the *North Carolina Historical Review* (for those who wished to have the two periodicals bound together). *Carolina Comments*, still published at present (although now quarterly), serves as the official newsletter of Archives and History, reports on current activities related to North Carolina history throughout the state, and often includes a feature article. In the fall of 1969 Archives and History, with the support of the Carolina Charter Corporation (successor to the Tercentenary Commission), was able to send a full-time researcher, Robert J. Cain, to England in search of materials of potential value to the Historical Publications Section's Colonial Records Project.

The National Historic Preservation Act of 1966 authorized the creation of the National Register for Historic Places and charged individual states with conducting "statewide surveys of their total physical historical assets and to nominate to the National Register properties that possess local, regional, statewide, and national significance." In North Carolina the survey was initiated in 1967—first with a private grant from the Smith Richardson Foundation and later with the first federal money allotted to the state from the Historic Preservation Fund. The first nominations from North Carolina were made in 1969. By the late 1970s most surveys received funding through matching subgrants from the State Historic Preservation Office (HPO) to local governments, colleges, and other organizations. Presently, as always, the State Historic Preservation Office carefully screens all nominations, making it possible for 99 percent of nominations from North Carolina to be listed on the Register. As of early 2000, more than 2,100 properties in the state were listed on the Register. The Historic Preservation Act also created a federal-state partnership that obligated the HPO to conduct reviews of federal- and state-funded projects to assess their potential impacts on historic properties and take action to minimize negative impacts whenever possible. As growth and development have increased in North Carolina, the reviews have mushroomed correspondingly.

The Tryon Palace complex continued to gain notoriety and to expand its properties in the 1960s. Free advertisement was secured on several occasions, such as when the palace was featured on the cover of the 1962 Esso road map of the Carolinas, selected as a site to be included in a special Coca-Cola sweepstakes in 1963, and highlighted in several magazines and newspapers published throughout the nation in 1964. In the latter year the Tryon Palace Commission purchased the Jones-Lipman House, situated on property adjacent to the palace. The commission repaired and restored the structure at no cost to the state, donating it for the use of the Tryon Palace complex. In November 1965 the New Bern Public Library offered the John Wright Stanly House as a gift to the Tryon Palace Commission. The house was built in the early 1780s for Stanly, a Revolutionary War patriot. It is believed that John Hawks, the architect who designed Tryon Palace, designed the Stanly House as well. The commission purchased a gas station situated on property adjoining the palace, then tore it down and moved the Stanly House to the site in December 1966. The palace hosted the first Tryon Palace Decorative Arts Symposium, now a program of considerable renown, in March 1969. The symposium, which highlights some aspect of the history of decorating, is still held in March of each year.

8

The Seventies: Department to Division

The nation's bicentennial commemoration of 1976 inspired a strong sense of community pride across the state. In large part a result of the Bicentennial, public interest in historical activities peaked during the 1970s, with many segments of Archives and History benefiting. Moreover, an exceptional number of published county histories appeared during the decade. The North Carolina American Revolution Bicentennial Commission, established by the General Assembly in 1967, produced a series of nineteen historical pamphlets related to the Revolutionary period in North Carolina. Some, such as *A Chronicle of North Carolina during the American Revolution, 1763-1789* and *The Black Experience in Revolutionary North Carolina*, both by Jeffrey J. Crow, remain in print. By 1973 the state committee served primarily as a resource for county organizations, which had been initiated at the request of Gov. Robert W. Scott in 1970.

Shortly after the nation's Bicentennial, the Division of Archives and History commemorated the seventy-fifth anniversary of the formation of the North Carolina Historical Commission. As one of the oldest public history organizations in the nation, the division sponsored a seminar with nationally recognized speakers addressing the various state programs. A publication titled *Public History in North Carolina, 1903-1978*, an outgrowth of the seminar, appeared the following year. The division issued the volume of essays, based on the speeches, in the hope that they would inspire other states' history organizations and public history professionals in general.

A 1971 administrative reorganization, driven by a gubernatorial edict to reduce the number of state agencies and to create a governor's cabinet with departmental secretaries, terminated Archives and History's independent departmental status. Effective February 1972, the former Department of Archives and History took its place under the newly created Department of Art, Culture, and History. From July 1972 until May 1973 the old department was called the Office of Archives and History (a name reclaimed in the wake of the reorganization of 2001). Further reorganization in May 1973 changed the departmental name to the Department of Cultural Resources, and the Office of Archives and History became the Division of Archives and History. As part of that revision,

Archives and History's governing body, the Executive Board of Archives and History, was renamed the North Carolina Historical Commission. The newly designated commission, unlike its predecessor created in 1903, was granted advisory status only; full statutory control of the agency was delegated to the secretary of Cultural Resources.

The historic sites acquired and developed by the state in the 1970s reflected the public's broadening historical interests. Negotiations with the owners of property encompassing Reed Gold Mine (the site in 1799 of the first authenticated discovery of gold in the United States) came to fruition in 1971. The state purchased 760 acres surrounding the mine from members of the Kelly family of Springfield, Ohio, who had used the property as a southern retreat for nearly eighty years. The family generously donated the most historically significant portion of the parcel, totaling seventy acres, to the state for use as a historic site. At the instigation of H. G. Jones, director of Archives and History at the time, citizens of Cabarrus County formed the nonprofit Gold History Corporation to raise funds and secure artifacts. The 1973 legislature appropriated money for the development of the site. Reconstruction of four hundred feet of tunnels and the construction of bridges, a visitor center, a maintenance building, a manager's residence, and a water and sewer system began. The site opened to the public in April 1977, and the National Park Service subsequently designated it a National Historic Landmark.

With H. G. Jones as their advocate, citizens of Durham formed the nonprofit Tobacco History Corporation in 1972. The organization, one of the most successful and active site support groups in North Carolina, raised money, acquired artifacts, published a newsletter, funded an artifact storage facility, and hired an

In 1973 Henry Brown, who directed underground restoration of Reed Gold Mine, took Historic Sites staff members Larry Misenheimer and Richard Knapp (shown at left here with Brown) deep into the abandoned mine.

Chapter Eight

exhibit designer. In 1999 members changed the name to the Duke Homestead Education and History Corporation to better represent the group's broader mission. Duke University in 1973 transferred to the state the Washington Duke Homestead, related buildings, and thirty-seven acres of land. Liggett and Myers Tobacco Company donated an adjoining 6 3/4 acres later that year. Archives and History took over operation of the site in 1974 with the intention of interpreting the history of tobacco, a vital part of North Carolina history and culture. The site and accompanying museum opened in May 1977.

Durham County was also home to Stagville, formerly the home of the Bennehan and Cameron families, whose holdings totaled nearly 30,000 acres and nine hundred slaves in 1860. Having owned the plantation property since the mid-1950s, the Liggett Group (successor to Liggett and Myers Tobacco Company), responding to the appeals of preservationists in the 1970s, donated seventy-one acres of real estate and the funds to develop the land as a historic site. Stagville Preservation Center opened in March 1977 as the nation's first state-owned center for the study and diffusion of knowledge in historic preservation. Since its inception, Stagville has offered a variety of educational seminars, workshops, and conferences on topics such as historic preservation, African American history, and botanical history. Many of Stagville's programs have been sponsored jointly with area universities and other public history organizations such as Old Salem and Colonial Williamsburg.

In 1974 the state entered into negotiations with the city of Asheville and Fred Wolfe, brother of writer Thomas Wolfe, to acquire the writer's boyhood home. A group of Asheville citizens had purchased the Wolfe boardinghouse in 1948—ten years after Thomas Wolfe's death—and operated it as a memorial to the novelist. The city of Asheville assumed operation of the site in 1958. Although the state acquired the property in July 1974, an ensuing budget cut prevented the General Assembly from appropriating the money necessary to rehabilitate it until a year later. Once rehabilitation commenced, the site was closed until 1976 to accommodate the work. In order to promote the development of a transportation-related historic site at the Southern Railway's former repair facility in Rowan County known as Spencer Shops, the Transportation History Corporation was formed in 1977. The 1979 legislature appropriated $1.25 million for the development of Spencer Shops, the largest single amount ever provided for a historic site. The first exhibits opened in 1983.

Far from remaining idle, existing state historic sites were expanding and maturing during the 1970s. In 1971 the Moore County Historical Association elected not to renew its lease of the House in the Horseshoe from the state, citing a perceived inability to maintain the property on a long-term basis. With an appropriation from the General Assembly for restoration and further capital improvements, Archives and History assumed control of the house on April 1, 1972. A similar chain of events transferred operation of the properties of Historic

The North Carolina Transportation Museum at Spencer Shops

Spencer Shops, which opened in 1896, was Southern Railway's largest repair facility. For years Southern employed between 2,500 and 3,000 workers in the Rowan County shops. The conversion from steam to diesel meant the demise of the facility. Southern began to lay off people through the 1950s; in 1960 the main shops were closed. The facility was completely shut down by 1979.

In the 1970s staff members of the Division of Archives and History envisioned a transportation museum but were hampered by problems of location and building size. The transfer of the Spencer property to the state gave the agency a prime location for such a facility, one convenient to travelers on Interstate 85. On July 1, 1977, the General Assembly authorized funds for the purchase of land and the stabilization of buildings. In September 1977, Southern Railway president L. Stanley Crane transferred 3.27 acres and three buildings at Spencer to the state of North Carolina. During the ensuing two years, Southern Railway donated the remaining fifty-seven acres and numerous buildings to the state.

The acquisition of Spencer Shops constituted a leap of faith on the part of state officials. Full-scale development of the massive complex would require the investment of millions in public and private funds. In 1978 a master plan was unveiled for the site. Hundreds of hours were devoted to removing debris and vegetation at the neglected facility. To assist the project, legislators in 1979 provided $1.25 million, the largest appropriation to a state historic site up to that time. Between July 1978 and June 1980, nearly four thousand people visited Spencer, even though it did not officially open until March 1983.

The first major exhibit—*People, Places, and Times*—opened in the former Master Mechanic's Office in 1983. The display covered the evolution of North Carolina's inland transportation. In 1990 an exhibit on automobiles titled *Bumper to Bumper* was placed in the former Flue Shop. In 1996, the centennial year of the shops, the Robert Julian Roundhouse opened to the public with approximately two dozen railroad locomotives and cars, more than five thousand artifacts, and a theater. The *Salisbury Post* referred to the roundhouse as "the crown jewel in an $8 million renovation effort." Upon the opening of the Roundhouse, the site's name was changed to the North Carolina Transportation Museum, which better reflected the diversifying interpretations. In 2000 Spencer Shops was the

---

Edenton to the state at about the same time. In 1972 the shelter for the CSS *Neuse* was completed at the Fort Caswell site in Kinston, giving the vessel some protection from the elements. In the mid-1970s, ruins of the most substantial surviving structure at Brunswick Town, St. Philip's Church, were stabilized, and federal funds were secured to do the same for the ruins of the earthen works of the Civil War-era Fort Anderson. During the mid-1970s, the Charles B. Aycock Birthplace revised its programming to offer more hands-on demonstrations, making the site more participatory in nature. The James K. Polk Birthplace changed its name to the Polk Memorial in 1977, at which time interpretations were broadened to include events from Polk's presidency. Following a systematic statewide survey and sampling of site visitors, it was determined that each site should host at least one special event per year (such as the Vance Birthplace's Pioneer Living Days) and should expand living history activities like hands-on demonstrations and military reenactments. By the late 1990s nearly one hundred

second most visited state historic site with 125,194 visitors. By 2001 the major focus was the rehabilitation of the Back Shop, which covers 200 yards in length, for exhibits. The projected cost was $30 million, with significant grants coming from the Department of Transportation and the Intermodal Surface Transportation Enhancements Act (ISTEA).

Spencer Shops' biggest assets are its nonprofit support group, the North Carolina Transportation History Foundation (formerly Corporation), and its corps of volunteers. The foundation, started in 1977, helps to raise funds and to obtain artifacts and restore them. Over the years it has acquired more than two million dollars' worth of artifacts. Volunteers, among them many former Southern Railway employees, have helped to restore and maintain railroad locomotives and cars. They also serve as docents and operate train rides.—*Dennis F. Daniels*

A bird's-eye view of the Southern Railway's Spencer Shops in the 1940s. The facility employed thousands of people during its operating period from 1896 to the 1960s. Spencer Shops is now the site of the North Carolina Transportation Museum.

such events occurred each year at the sites. The programs, while requiring substantial staff and volunteer resources, in some cases drew thousands of visitors to particular sites in a few days' time.

Activity at historic sites aside, the Division of Archives and History extended its presence through new services and new office locations during the 1970s. In an effort to bolster communication between both large and small historical organizations in the state, the division in 1975 began coordinating and administering the Federation of North Carolina Historical Societies. The Federation, an ongoing program, offers services such as a quarterly bulletin, training workshops of interest to historical groups, and a no-interest loan fund for organizations wishing to publish a local history or organize fund-raising events. In September 1978 the division opened a Western Office in Asheville. Most facets of Archives and History are represented at that outpost. There, staff members host and assist with a variety of educational programs on topics such as historical editing and restoration. The Western Office has rendered assistance over the years to a wide range of historical organizations and has made consultation in museum work, historic preservation, and records management readily available to citizens of western North Carolina.

The Western North Carolina Office of the Division of Archives a History opened in the Oteen Center near As[l]ville in October 1978. The building is picture[d] here during exterior restoration in 1986. In September 1993 the o[f] relocated to Biltmore Village.

Bringing aid and advice in the realm of historic preservation to residents of the state's northern coastal region, the Northeastern Historic Places Office (NEHPO) opened in December 1978 in Edenton's historic Barker House. Its staff offered planning, evaluation, and program design to nonprofit historic sites and organizations in the northeastern counties. The office also administered a program of matching grants. On uncertain financial footing from the outset, NEHPO was closed in 1995 when its funding was cut from the state budget.

When the Division of Historic Sites and Museums was split into two separate sections in 1974, John D. Ellington assumed the role of museum administrator—a position he would occupy for twenty years. The Museum of History expanded in July 1979 with the acquisition of its first regional service branch. The Museum of the Albemarle in Elizabeth City had operated independently since 1967 as one of four planned regional museum service branches. The goal of maintaining such branches was to offer better educational services to citizens of and visitors to the more remote locations in the state and to assist other local museums in all aspects of operation. Interpretation at the Museum of the Albemarle remained focused on the settlers and events of that region.

In 1975, under the leadership of Larry E. Tise, who became director of the Division of Archives and History that year, the agency underwent a major reorganization. The changes were intended to emphasize management and administrative functions. Noteworthy was the creation of two new sections: State Capitol/Visitor Services and Historic Preservation. The State Capitol came under the control of the division with an extensive interior renovation on the cusp of completion. That project concluded in 1976 when the building's original furnishings and reproduction carpets were installed in the two legislative chambers. (The Capitol's original 1840 legislative chairs were replaced with reproductions in 1994.) Because of the renovations, the State Capitol had been closed to the public for nine months, but it was reopened in time for the Bicentennial. Shortly thereafter, managers initiated a docent training program, which drew volunteers from civic organizations and the public at large. In January 1977, effective as of his inauguration as governor, James B. Hunt Jr. resumed the practice of maintaining an office in the Capitol building (Gov. James E. Holshouser Jr. had maintained headquarters in the Administration Building for four years during the Capitol renovations).

The State Capitol joined the Division of Archives and History in 1975 at which time exterior and interior renovations of the building were under way. This 1972 photograph shows consulting architect Orin Bullock Jr. taking paint samples from the rotunda of the building.

Largely because of the Bicentennial fervor, historic preservation enjoyed a surge in interest as communities focused on adaptive restoration projects—that is, making use of old buildings for new purposes. The small eastern North Carolina town of Washington created a convention center and arts council facility out of an old railroad station, and in Lexington the Greek Revival courthouse became the county history museum. Another motivating factor in the sudden popularity of historic preservation was the Tax Reform Act of 1976, which included a federal investment tax credit for qualifying rehabilitations of income-producing properties. The State Historic Preservation Office (HPO) was designated as the state agency responsible for reviewing applications from the owners of buildings interested in pursuing the tax credit by complying with required rehabilitation standards. Carr Mill Mall in Carrboro was the first property to take advantage of the program in North Carolina. In the mid-1970s the federal government also made funds available for state historic preservation projects. The HPO distributed that money to local governments and groups in the form of subgrants. Projects funded by such subgrants included architectural and archaeological surveys, preservation planning, and building restoration. In 1980 the federal government stipulated that 10 percent of the funds apportioned by the states must be given to Certified Local Governments—those designated as having federally and state-approved preservation programs.

In 1976 and 1977 the HPO's Survey and Planning Branch conducted an architectural survey of twenty-nine counties in the Tar-Neuse River basin. The project culminated in a single report covering the region and summarizing old and new fieldwork. During the 1976-1978 biennium, the branch, in cooperation with North Carolina State University's School of Design and the Administrative Office of the Courts, conducted a systematic survey of courthouses in North Carolina. The study, which called attention to the preservation of the historic structures, ultimately led to more than sixty courthouses being listed on the National Register. Until 1978 branch staff conducted most of the survey fieldwork, but thereafter it was handled by consultants working for local groups that received matching grants administered by the branch.

Late in the decade, goals in the realms of archaeology and historic preservation were aided by passage of the state's Historic Preservation and Conservation Agreements Act, which provided "a strong legal basis for the donation and selling of easements to protect natural and cultural resources." Archives and History, the state Attorney General's Office, and a consortium of other groups planned an easement program to conserve historic properties and resources. The participating agencies also developed a manual on easements and hosted two conferences on the subject.

In September 1973 the Division of Archives and History created the Archaeology Section, removing most archaeological duties from the Museum of History and the Historic Sites Section. (Four years later the new section was combined with Historic Preservation to form the Archaeology and Historic Preservation Section.) In October 1973 Archives and History claimed an important legal victory. The previous year, private salvors had removed two cannon from the Roanoke River at Fort Branch in Martin County. The sheriff of Martin County seized the weapons before the men could leave the area. An ensuing legal battle ended in November 1973 when the state court of appeals, citing General Statute 121, Article 3, which had been enacted to protect archaeological resources located in North Carolina, ruled that the cannon were the legal property of the state and must be returned to state custody. The ruling established that abandoned material in navigable waterways reverts to state ownership after ten years. The preserved cannon are on display at Fort Branch in Hamilton.

During the 1974-1976 biennium, the Archaeology Section developed an environmental assessment program—one of the most functional and effective in the nation—with which to evaluate the potential impact of construction projects on archaeological resources prior to the issuance of funds or permits. During the period, the staff reviewed five thousand projects, resulting in the conservation of nearly two thousand archaeologically significant sites. One notable example was a month-long study of the New River basin during which archaeologists identified two hundred sites, although only eighteen had been known previously. Near the end of the decade, public interest in the archaeology program was so strong that the branch instituted evening work and training sessions at the branch laboratory in Raleigh. The evening sessions eventually became the bimonthly "Volunteer Lab Night," especially popular with area college students.

In August 1973 the Archaeology Branch (which became the Archaeology Section one month later) participated in the official identification of the remains of the renowned Civil War ironclad USS *Monitor*. In January 1975 the U.S. secretary of commerce designated the wreck site, located sixteen miles off the coast of Cape Hatteras, as the nation's first National Marine Sanctuary. Two years later the division, the National Oceanic and Atmospheric Administration (NOAA), and the Harbor Branch Foundation jointly sponsored reconnaissance and recovery operations at the *Monitor* Marine Sanctuary. The Archaeology Section coordinated the drafting of guidelines for future research and recovery operations related to the *Monitor*. In 1983, with NOAA managing the *Monitor* Marine Sanctuary, the state office resolved to limit future involvement with the site to the review of project proposals.

Economic woes of the early and mid-1970s hit the Historical Publications Section hard. The *North Carolina Historical Review* could no longer be printed on Perma-life acid-free paper because the cost was prohibitive, and production of documentary volumes was so costly that it was difficult to recover printing costs. As a result, documentaries were nearly priced out of the market. Budgetary problems led the section to institute shipping and handling charges on materials in November 1977. Shortly thereafter, chain stores such as Belk's and Walden Books began selling some of the departmental publications, improving sales figures and increasing public awareness of the program. In February 1979 the Historical Publications Section released *Journal of a "Secesh Lady": The Diary of Catherine Ann Devereaux Edmondston, 1860-1866*, edited by Beth G. Crabtree and James W. Patton, a project that had been in the works for decades. The initial printing of one thousand copies was sold by late fall, with the second thousand selling almost as quickly. The volume, still in print, is an especially useful resource for those researching nineteenth-century North Carolina.

Between July 1, 1970, and June 30, 1974, all records management responsibilities relating to the creation, utilization, and maintenance of state records were transferred from the State Records Center to the Systems Management Division of the Department of Administration. Many positions were transferred to that department, and many that remained were redefined. Responsibilities that remained with the State Records Center included conducting records inventories, creating records disposition schedules, managing the records center facility, and operating the microfilming program. The return of the duties to Archives and History in 1974 helped to restore the original mission of the former State

The fifth volume of the *Colonial Records* series, *North Carolina Higher-Court Records, 1709-1723,* edited by William Price Jr., was published in 1977. Pictured with Price (*second from left*) at the formal presentation ceremony: Sara W. Hodgkins, secretary, Department of Cultural Resources; Robert Cain, Price's successor; and Memory F. Mitchell, Historical Publications administrator.

Records Section. In 1971 the Local Records Section, having completed its original objective of inventorying and microfilming permanently valuable or essential county records prior to 1959, initiated a new phase to microfilm those records created *since* 1959. When, during the 1972-1974 biennium, state records analysts discovered that the rate of compliance with records schedules in the agencies was only 29 percent, they increased the number of site visits and launched a program offering orientation tours of the Records Center and seminars on records management. The efforts resulted in a dramatic reduction in the number of records created and a corresponding increase in the number of records destroyed, saving the state money and office space.

During the 1970-1972 biennium, the renovation of the Records Center Building on Lane Street, begun in 1969, was completed. The shelves in the building were 92 percent full within ninety days of the renovation. While a sorely needed new records center facility was funded and built, budgetary restrictions left the building with significantly less shelving than originally planned. That building, on Blount Street, was completed in 1975, but because of a budgetary freeze the relocation of some 75,000 cubic feet of records was suspended for several months. It took thirty-five months—until October 1978—to accomplish the task of transferring the records. Fortunately no records were damaged in February 1977 when a steam valve burst early one morning. The building's air handlers and dampers did not shut down in time to prevent the release of 300-degree steam through the heating, ventilation, and air conditioning system. Two microfilm cameras and many light fixtures and ceiling tiles were lost. The internal tube system and the ventilation system were destroyed. Records containers were damaged and box labels fell off. Problems involving humidity and temperature control plagued the building for eighteen months as a result of the steam valve's rupture.

The Archives and Records Section, formed in 1972, implemented a comprehensive educational program during the 1972-1974 biennium, spearheaded by C. F. W. (Fred) Coker. The staff organized institutes and workshops on the resources available at the State Archives and how to use them. They constructed and circulated small traveling exhibits designed to draw interest to specific collections. Among the diverse topics covered by the traveling exhibits was the First Provincial Congress at New Bern, Secretary of State trademarks, and the construction of Central Prison. The exhibits, in addition to providing learning experiences for young archivists, were excellent outreach tools. It was at this time that the section initiated its first computer indexing project. Entering information from the county-by-county marriage bond abstracts onto computer punch cards, the staff was able to generate a statewide index. Also during this biennium the section assumed responsibility for the division's iconographic materials, including those held by the Museum of History. Significant nontextual collections have been accumulated ever since, including negatives, original prints, motion picture film, sound recordings, and videotapes.

In 1974 an organized group stole numerous documents from the State Archives, which were later advertised for sale by a manuscript dealer who, in turn, cooperated with the state to solve the case and return the materials. That theft compelled the Archives and Records Section to implement strict security measures. Also that year, the state archivist became involved in a precedent-setting court case that exacted the return of other treasures of the state's documentary history.

Just as the Archives staff sought to teach the public about research and resources, the community college system introduced as extension courses a curriculum on local history and genealogy. In response to a generous appropriation for equipment from the 1973 legislature, the Department of Community Colleges requested that Archives and History identify a "core collection" of important records on microfilm for each county, including but not limited to wills, estates, deeds, and court minutes. The records were ones already on microfilm in the security vault within the agency. The community colleges and local libraries then could order copies of the film for students taking the courses. The offering was so popular that the State Archives was inundated with microfilm orders and was obliged to purchase new microfilm duplicating equipment in order to avoid exhausting its supply of silver-film stock.

While the Archives courses and the Bicentennial accelerated interest in genealogy, the January 1977 broadcast of *Roots*, the television miniseries based on Alex Haley's fact-based novel of the same name, caused interest in the subject to soar. The demand for reference services in the Archives Search Room rose by 28 percent, and mail inquiries were up by 17 percent. So much assistance was needed at the reference desk that arrangement and description work languished as staff members were called upon to help researchers. With that work, as well as holdings maintenance, suffering, the secretary of Cultural Resources approved the closing of the Search Room on Mondays effective July 1, 1978. Staff continued to work on Mondays, giving them the opportunity to respond to requests

North Carolina v. B. C. West Jr.:
Modern Replevin Precedent

In May 1974, archivist Paul Hoffman learned of an upcoming New York auction scheduled to include a 1790 letter from George Washington to the governor and council of state of North Carolina. With confirmation that the letter was still available, the state began negotiating for its return. According to Thornton W. Mitchell, then state archivist, "there were no modern precedents supporting the civil recovery or replevin of public records in case law." Nevertheless, the Attorney General's Office recommended that recovery of the letter be pursued.

Separately, in June 1974 the State Archives discovered a major theft of state documents. In hopes of locating some of the stolen records, staff members began scrutinizing catalogs offering manuscripts for sale. In January 1975 archivist George Stevenson noticed two items—indictments signed in 1767 and 1768 respectively by William Hooper, later a signer of the Declaration of Independence—for sale by B. C. West Jr., an autograph dealer in Elizabeth City. Although the two items West offered for sale were not casualties of the 1974 theft, they

Thornton Mitchell joined the staff of the Department of Archives and History in 1961. He served as State Archivist from 1973 until his retirement in 1981. Mitchell was responsible for pursuing the *State of North Carolina v. B.C. West Jr.* replevin case.

involving collections, prepare finding aids, and answer correspondence. In February 1978 a nonprofit support group known as the Friends of the Archives was established. The Friends continue to provide volunteer time, financial support of archival and records management projects, and sponsorship of workshops, internships, and other services on behalf of the State Archives.

The Museum of History formed its own support organization, the Museum of History Associates, in the fall of 1975. Twenty-five years later, the Associates included members from all one hundred counties, and total membership stood at fifteen thousand people. The organization's principal objective is to advance the activities of the main museum and its regional branches. The Associates have provided funds for the purchase and conservation of artifacts; underwritten exhibits, programs, and publications; and sponsored the grand opening of the new museum building and other educational and fund-raising events. Currently the group operates the museum's gift shop.

The Museum of History mounted several important exhibits during the 1970s. It acquired the gun shop of David Marshall "Carbine" Williams, moved it to the museum, and reconstructed it in exact accordance with its original appearance. The museum had to alter its exhibit layouts in the Jones Street location in

were, nevertheless, bona fide public records that had fallen out of the state's custody. Assisting in what had become a division-wide effort to seek the return of the eighteenth-century indictments, Colonial Records Project editor William S. Price Jr. investigated the historical background of the common law in relation to public records. Robert J. Cain, colonial records researcher stationed in London, procured copies of British Records related to replevin—the legal process of recovering goods or chattels claimed to be wrongfully taken or detained—of documents.

In a strategic move not fully appreciated at the time, Mitchell decided to pursue the Hooper indictments through litigation. Many believed that if the state lost the West case, then surely it would fail to reclaim the prized Washington letter. Furthermore, Mitchell set himself up as the main antagonist in the matter. It was possible that the case could drag on for years, and he knew that his career had peaked. Thus he was willing to put his professional reputation on the line, knowing that if he succeeded, then the State Archives (if not all state archives) would benefit, and if not, he would retire in 1981 in hopes of minimizing the negative impact on the agency.

North Carolina v. B. C. West Jr. was heard for two days in the Pasquotank County Court. At the close, Judge John Webb ruled that while the law favored the state, his decision would uphold the position of the defendant because of the age of the documents and the lack of information as to when and how they left the state's custody. The state appealed and won the case the following year. West appealed that decision to the North Carolina Supreme Court, which in June 1977 in a five-to-two decision upheld the ruling of the court of appeals. The state's progress in the matter of the 1790 Washington letter in New York wavered, but once the West case was decided, the competing claims for ownership of the letter were concluded promptly in an out-of-court agreement. Thornton Mitchell flew to New York in July 1977 to escort the letter personally. Mitchell enjoyed the one great irony of the replevin matters of the late 1970s. Who alerted Paul Hoffman to the rare personally handwritten Washington letter that initiated the events? It was none other than B. C. West Jr.—*Ansley Herring Wegner*

---

order to accommodate Williams's full workshop. Williams also donated weapon prototypes for display. The exhibit opened June 22, 1971, and remained in its permanent location until it was dismantled and moved to the museum's new facility in 1999. In November 1975, in an effort to increase the visibility of black history in its exhibits, the museum opened a display on furniture maker Thomas Day, his furniture, and his craftsmanship and published an accompanying exhibit catalog. Although small in scale, the exhibit focused national attention on the museum and the African American craftsman. The first major exhibit devoted to minority history was *The Black Presence in North Carolina* (1978). Funded in part by a grant in the amount of $76,000 from the National Endowment for the Humanities, the exhibit encompassed 1,900 square feet of exhibit space and was two years in the planning. Aside from exhibits, the museum delved into alternative-education presentations through its "Month of Sundays" programs. The monthly offerings included travel films and lectures and were quite popular, averaging one hundred participants at each event.

Archives and History saw the dawn of automation during the 1970s. The Archaeology and Historic Preservation Section implemented the Cultural Resources Evaluation Program (CREP) after the 1978 legislature provided an

The Black Presence in North Carolina: *Another Side of the Story*

In the fall of 1978, the North Carolina Museum of History (NCMOH) opened its first major exhibit devoted to black North Carolinians. This groundbreaking exhibit, which extended the story from African origins to 1900, constituted a concerted effort by Archives and History to present the contributions of African Americans in the context of state and national events. *Carolina Comments* noted at the time that "the true impact of the 'The Black Presence in North Carolina' on the public will be the illumination of a part of the state's history too little understood and too frequently ignored."

A grant in the amount of $76,000 from the National Endowment for the Humanities helped make the exhibit possible. The acquisition of artifacts related to black North Carolinians, an aspect of the state's history about which the museum's holdings were few, posed a challenge. Curator Rodney Barfield, who is white, initially encountered distrust. He told the Raleigh *News and Observer* that once people overcame their concerns, "they just opened up and gave me lovely information and supporting documents." Many new items became part of the permanent collection, while others were loaned for display. The exhibit was divided into nine sections: African Heritage, Revolution, The Written Word, The Spoken Word, Free Blacks, Bronze Men in Blue, Political Leadership, Education, and Business World. Almost 128,000 people visited the display over the course of its year-long run. The media provided extensive coverage. An editorial in the *Greensboro Record* indicated that "a state which has long neglected the history and contributions of its black citizens is making a graceful, if partial, amends now in Raleigh."

The Black Presence in North Carolina, a major exhibit at the Museum of History, opened in September 1978. Almost 128,000 people attended the exhibit over the course of its year-long run.

The Black Presence was not limited to the exhibit in Raleigh. The NCMOH placed a scaled-down version in its "Mobile Museum of History," which traveled to schools and other public areas. At least 43,000 people climbed aboard. A book and a recording grew out of the project. The book, which carried the same name as the exhibit, featured four essays about African American leadership, religion, literature, and music in North Carolina. The album, *Eight-Hand Sets and Holy Steps,* was a compilation that featured secular and inspirational African American music dating from the slave era to the 1930s. Folklorist Glenn Hinson recorded the music in the field.

The exhibit and its related projects left an impact beyond the NCMOH. Other organizations mounted their own African American exhibits, and the museum offered assistance in a number of cases. It developed spin-off exhibits to appear at other places; examples included a photographic display based on the exhibit for display in the North Carolina Mutual Life Insurance Building in Durham. The insurance company issued a 1979 calendar with *The Black Presence* as its theme. In 1979 the North Carolina chapter of the National Association for the Advancement of Colored People sponsored one hundred radio spots related to people and events featured in the exhibit. In the quarter-century since the exhibit was mounted, the story of African Americans in North Carolina has become better known and a recognized part of the larger story of the state.—*Dennis F. Daniels*

David Marshall ("Carbine") Williams's Cumberland County workshop was dismantled and reassembled as an exhibit in the Museum of History. The floor plan of the museum's space in the Archives and History/State Library Building had to be altered in order to accommodate the exhibit, which opened in June 1971.

appropriation for hardware, software, and an additional employee to implement the system. Initially the work involved the creation of standardized forms, followed by transcription, proofing, and data entry of information derived from the forms. During the same biennium, Larry G. Misenheimer, then assistant administrator of the Historic Sites Section, installed the Cultural Materials Accession System (CUMAS), a data processing system for accessions. Preliminary use of CUMAS was limited to that section, but by the end of the biennium both Tryon Palace and the Museum of History had adopted it. One problem the museum encountered was that most accession records prior to 1967 were incomplete. At the time, data entry was expected to take about fifteen years to complete. Although data entry still has not been completed, CUMAS contained 69,000 artifact records in 1998 when the museum switched to a more user-friendly system called "Re:Discovery." Likewise, Historic Sites and Tryon Palace presently utilize Re:Discovery.

9

The Eighties: Automation in the Service of History

Following Archives and History's tentative entry into the computer age in the late 1970s, computerization in the 1980s was more comprehensive and enduring. The Archaeology and Historic Preservation Section expanded its use of the Cultural Resources Evaluation Program (CREP), both in-house for review purposes and externally by architectural historians, universities, state agencies, and developers needing site-specific information. Computer terminals for data entry into CREP were installed at the home office and at the Underwater Archaeology Unit at Kure Beach. Within Historic Sites Larry Misenheimer planned and implemented the first stage of his computerized Sites Assets Management System for use in budgeting, scheduling, and analyzing assets. After becoming administrator of the section in 1985, Misenheimer continued his push for computerization with his Historical Information Cataloging and Tracking System (HICATS), created initially for inventorying an extensive collection of North Caroliniana donated to the state by coastal historian David Stick. (That collection formed the foundation for the subsequent establishment in Manteo of the David Stick Collection at the Outer Banks History Center in the mid-1980s.) Although other offices within the division adopted HICATS, the system subsequently proved inadequate.

After two years of deliberative planning, the Archives and Records Section implemented a computer automation program in 1984. Arlon Kemple, computer specialist with the Department of Cultural Resources, working in conjunction with Archives and Records staff, developed FAIDS (short for Finding Aids). The computer system was to provide for the Archives' immediate internal needs, such as record location, and eventually an online system. In 1988 the name of the program was changed to MARS (Manuscript and Archives Reference System). By that time the system was being used to describe all state agency records and to print out folder labels and finding aids. Also by 1988 the State Records Center was conducting most daily operations with the use of computers. Staff used them for inventory control, including the location and shelving of materials, and for printing records retention and disposition schedules. In April

1990 Search Room patrons began making use of the finding aid aspect of the computer system.

In 1984 the Historical Publications Section purchased two word processors, using budgeted receipts, and four staff members were trained in the use of the machines. That year the introduction and the index to volume 7 of the *Colonial Records* and the index to volume 7 of *The Papers of William Alexander Graham* were prepared in-house using the new word processors. Such technology helped to reduce the selling prices of some publications by reducing production costs.

Catherine J. Morris (*second from left*) demonstrated the agency's automated finding-aid system, then known as FAIDS (an acronym for Finding Aids), to a group of visiting archivists in 1987. The next year the name of the program changed to MARS, for Manuscript and Archives Reference System.

Volume 6 of the *Graham Papers* had sold for $29.50, whereas volume 7, which was approximately the same length, was priced at $25.00.

In May 1987 the Museum of History purchased desktop publishing equipment for use in generating the *Tar Heel Junior Historian* and the museum's newsletter, *Crossroads*. Staff members were able to use the computer system to create teacher-resource materials, exhibit flyers, publicity materials, and other documents. In keeping with R. D. W. Connor's conviction that the state historical agency should promote North Carolina history in the schools, the Division of Archives and History worked with the State Board of Education during the 1980-1982 biennium to restore North Carolina history to the eighth-grade public school curriculum. Members of the Tar Heel Junior Historian Association staff played a pivotal role in effecting the return of the course in the fall of 1983, after an absence of ten years. With North Carolina history as a required course once again, the division benefited through increased sales of publications and expanded visitation at museums and state historic sites.

Despite a budget shortfall experienced in the early 1980s, educational programs diversified within the division. In 1980 the Archaeology Branch instituted a volunteer training course, offering a twenty-four-hour surveyor certification program. Public participation in state archaeological projects was encouraged and appreciated. By the mid-1980s, the volunteer program had operations based in Raleigh, at Fort Fisher, and at the Western Office in Asheville. Toward the end of the decade, the branch was obliged to initiate new projects for volunteers simply to meet public demand.

In other outreach activities, numerous educational workshops were offered in the 1980s. The State Archives offered several popular genealogical seminars, in which staff members were instrumental in making preparations and local arrangements or in preparing and delivering lectures. In Asheville and other mountain communities, the Western Office hosted a variety of lectures and programs for educators, students, and historical organizations. Tryon Palace continued to offer its perennially popular decorative arts and gardening workshops. In 1985 the Museum of the Albemarle initiated a lunchtime lecture series called "A Taste of History." A program was presented once a month at a downtown location in an effort to encourage participation by members of the business community.

The Historic Sites Section likewise was active on the educational front in the 1980s. In the early part of the decade staff began distributing packets to teachers for use before and after visits to some sites. The packets helped students and teachers make the most of their field trips. The History Bowl quiz competition expanded into a statewide tournament in 1984. By that time about eighty schools participated at six of the sites in competitions to select teams to advance to the state finals, held in Raleigh. By the mid-1980s the section had resolved to open at the former location of the Alice Freeman Palmer Memorial Institute in Sedalia (Guilford County) a new historic site devoted to the history of African Americans in North Carolina, as well as larger themes in the realms of education and social history. To oversee planning for the new facility, to be known as the Charlotte Hawkins Brown Memorial, the section hired as project director Annette Gibbs, who oversaw site research and planning, wrote and narrated radio features on black history that were distributed to more than 280 stations, coordinated a black-history awareness conference, and helped produce a traveling exhibit on the history of African Americans in North Carolina.

Another Historic Sites-related educational project, six years in the making, culminated with the 1983 publication of the five-volume series, *The Way We Lived in North Carolina*. The books, underwritten by a major NEH grant and published by the University of North Carolina Press, focused on the lives of ordinary people and highlighted North Carolina historic sites, as well as other places of historical interest in the state, as backdrops to a narrative social history. The amply illustrated volumes were geared toward the general public and travelers. In 1984 the series won the American Historical Association's James Harvey Robinson Prize.

Historic sites evolved in the 1980s as managers added aspects of living history to their programs. Whether through costumed interpreters, historical dramas, or demonstrations of historical skills, many sites benefited from the emphasis on education. Some sites, such as Bentonville Battleground and the *Elizabeth II*, added costumed interpreters for the first time. After conducting considerable research, Tryon Palace updated its costumes to make them more historically accurate. The palace also offered a variety of popular historical dramas, ranging from simple interactive monologues to those featuring a small cast. Tryon Palace's "Colonial Skills" tours, featuring such handiwork as spinning, weaving, candle-dipping, blacksmithing, and hearthside cooking, appealed particularly to young visitors.

In the 1980s Tryon Palace witnessed a significant increase in the number of school groups that participated in the Colonial Skills Tours. This group is touring the Palace kitchen.

In the early 1980s the House in the Horseshoe reconstructed on the property a loom house, in which volunteers demonstrated period spinning and weaving techniques. About the same time, the Charles B. Aycock Birthplace began interpreting period agriculture through livestock and farming demonstrations by volunteers.

In 1984 a Winston-Salem citizens' group, concerned that knowledge of Piedmont agriculture was rapidly declining, proposed creation of a living history farm. The Hauser Farm, in an undeveloped part of Pilot Mountain State Park, was chosen to interpret farms of the northwest Piedmont in the 1900–1910 period. The citizens' group, as well as members of the General Assembly and Cultural Resources staff involved in the project, agreed that the farm should interpret the general middle-class farmer, rather than the Hauser family specifically. They chose to name the facility Horne Creek Living Historical Farm, for a waterway that ran through the property. The farmstead was designated a state historic site in October 1987. African American cultural traditions, including the

The Horne Creek Living Historical Farm, located near Winston-Salem, became a state historic site in 1987. The farm is dedicated to preserving and demonstrating farming methods from the turn of the twentieth century.

reenactment of a slave wedding, were highlighted at the first Somerset Place Homecoming in 1986. The event, hosted by the site for descendants of slaves who had lived and worked at the plantation, received international attention. It was the first major program of its type to be offered at a former plantation. The homecoming, held again in 2001, was a commemoration and validation of the work performed by the slaves in the South and a celebration of African American culture with activities, demonstrations, and dramatic performances.

Approximately 2,500 participants attended the Somerset Place Homecoming and toured the grounds of the former plantation in Washington County.

As a result of severe budget cuts, Archives and History started the 1980s with an overall staff reduction of 5 percent. The Archaeology and Historic Preservation Section sustained the most significant setback, losing five full-time and all part-time positions—a 25 percent cut in personnel. The state-funded portion of the operating budget was reduced by nearly $500,000, which resulted in curtailed travel and significant reductions in purchases of equipment and supplies. The section's federal allocations were reduced even more drastically. By the close of the 1982-1984 biennium, the economic situation had improved. Unfortunately, the section continued to be plagued with budgetary problems until the mid-1980s because the federal funding level remained lower than it had been at the start of the decade. The section was fortunate to have had such an active volunteer base to help with the workload during the early part of the decade. Also because of budgetary reductions, the Historic Sites Section was compelled to adopt winter hours from November through March. For the winter months, hours were reduced from fifty-two hours a week over seven days to thirty-three hours over six days. The winter-hours schedule remains in place at present.

In 1981 two amendments to the Indian Antiquities Law of 1935 directly affected the Archaeology Branch. The changes resulted from two years of development and discussion among concerned organizations such as the Commission of Indian Affairs, the Governor's Archaeological Advisory Committee, and the North Carolina Archaeological Council. The Archaeological Resources Protection Act (NCGS Ch. 70, Article 5) simply clarified the definition of such resources and strengthened the state's ability to protect them. The Unmarked Burial and

Chapter Nine

Human Skeletal Remains Protection Act (NCGS Ch. 70, Article 6) extended protection to all unmarked human burials in the state except for those on federally owned or controlled land and prohibited their disturbance by all except qualified archaeologists. (Several additional aspects of the legislation established procedures to be followed in the handling and reinterment of human remains.) Also affecting the Archaeology Branch was a 273 percent increase in the number of visits made to archaeological sites during the 1982-1984 biennium. Two factors were cited for the increase: an elevated volume of environmental review projects and a heightened public awareness of the duties of the Archaeology Branch. The huge increase in visitation functioned as a form of outreach and attracted a large number of vol-

unteers, which the branch sorely needed. The State Highway Funding Act of 1989 created even more environmental review work for the Archaeology and Historic Preservation Section. In anticipation of an expected increase in demand for its services, the section's Administrative Branch held workshops in May and August of that year to explain the environmental review process to consulting engineering companies and architectural historians carrying out survey work for the Department of Transportation.

The Outer Banks History Center in Manteo opened in May 1989. The facility, adjacent to the visitor center for the *Elizabeth II* State Historic Site, is now part of the complex known as Roanoke Island Festival Park.

With the four hundredth anniversary of the Roanoke voyages (1584–1587) in mind, Gov. James B. Hunt Jr. in 1978 appointed members to a body known as America's Four Hundredth Anniversary Committee; the governor named as chairman of the committee H. G. Jones, former director of Archives and History. Hunt was particularly interested in the idea of creating a replica sixteenth-century sailing vessel for the event. In September of that year the committee created the nonprofit American Quadricentennial Corporation to assist and finance the various programs, with emphasis on the proposed ship. By 1980 the group had privately raised $650,000 to build the vessel, known as the *Elizabeth II*; the legislature responded two years later with a $1.4 million appropriation to develop the ship as a state historic site. In July 1982 craftsmen began constructing the *Elizabeth II* by hand. Her Royal Highness Princess Anne of Great Britain dedicated the ship and site on July 13, 1984. The Outer Banks History Center, constructed as an addition to the *Elizabeth II* visitor center, opened in the spring of 1989. It continues to expand its holdings and is of particular interest to those conducting research on topics pertaining to coastal North Carolina. The management of the replica ship was transferred from the Historic Sites Section to the Roanoke Island Commission, an autonomous agency within the Department of Cultural Resources, in December 1995.

The Division of Archives and History expanded further with the October 1983 opening of its Eastern Office of Archives and History in Greenville's historic Humber House. During the first year of operation, staff held public information meetings related to historic preservation and other Archives and History programs. The Eastern Office and East Carolina University's public history program cosponsored at the historic Humber House in Greenville an exhibit on Civil War blockade-runners.

Constructed in 1895, the Robert Lee Humber House in Greenville, North Carolina, currently serves as the headquarters for the Eastern Office of Archives and History. This 1905 image depicts the Humber family.

The Museum of History expanded services to western North Carolina in July 1982 with the addition of the regional Mountain Gateway Museum and Western Regional Museum Service Center at Old Fort. Visitation at the museum and community use of the facility and grounds increased markedly during the early part of the decade. Requests for assistance from the service center involved design, implementation, and construction projects. The photography lab at Old Fort expanded in the winter of 1982, providing valuable assistance and services to museums and other facilities in the area. In the early 1980s, the Western Office published a brochure giving details about various local history museums in the mountain region, along with a map showing the location of each museum. The brochure helped those facilities attract interested tourists who otherwise might not have learned of them. In the mid- 1980s, the staff of the Western Office encouraged the creation and development of oral history projects and assisted local citizens in conducting interviews. Staff members organized their own series of interviews with notable area craftsmen.

The Division of Archives and History's third regional history museum and service center, funded in 1983, was located in Fayetteville. The service center opened as an office in September of that year. Renovations to an existing building, the old Highsmith-Rainey nursing dormitory adjacent to the remains of a Civil War-era arsenal, were funded in 1984. The facility, leased to the state at no cost for twenty years, required extensive interior refurbishing. During the 1984-1986 biennium, floor plans were drawn and exhibits were planned for the facility, which became known as the Museum of the Cape Fear. Artifacts important to the region, notably Scottish items and turpentine tools, were acquired. In April 1986 the museum began hosting a three-day weekend military encampment. Featured as part of other programs were various living history demonstrations, including cooking, crafts, and music. The Museum of the Cape Fear opened in June 1988. The museum complex consists of a three-story main building; the late-Victorian-era Poe House, acquired in December 1986; and a surviving component of a Civil War-era Federal arsenal owned by the city of Fayetteville and assigned to the museum for use as an interpretive center. The museum's service center provided on-site assistance to many historic and educational organizations throughout the 1980s.

Not to be outdone by its branch museums in the 1980s, the main Museum of History in Raleigh was expanding physically and creatively. During the 1984-1986 biennium, plans were taking shape to relocate the Museum of History into the old Museum of Art space on Morgan Street. In early 1985 that plan was dropped in favor of erecting a new building adjacent to the Bicentennial Mall between the State Capitol and the Legislative Building. At the time, three reasons were advanced for the abrupt change in plans: a new master plan called for a cultural center within the government complex; the state Department of Transportation requested use of the old Museum of Art for needed office space; and legislators wanted additional public parking near their building. A ceremonial groundbreaking for the new building, complete with ceremonial jackhammering by James G. Martin and James B. Hunt Jr., took place in June 1988; construction did not begin until the following April. Contributing to the museum's increased visibility was the massive publicity that surrounded its first international exhibition, *Raleigh & Roanoke* (March 1985). Following seven years of planning in connection with America's Four Hundredth Anniversary, the exhibit consisted of more than 130 documents, maps, and artifacts from a number of British repositories. The museum's hours of operation were extended to accommodate a tremendous increase in visitation, and the building was given twenty-four-hour security protection. During the exhibit's three-month run, more than ninety thousand people viewed it.

Among other expansion projects, the Tryon Palace Restoration Complex in the mid-1980s leased a property that offered new opportunities for historical interpretation. The New Bern Academy building, completed in 1809 and in use as a school until 1970, was the first school chartered in North Carolina (a tax was levied for its support in 1766). The palace complex developed a museum in the facility to interpret the history of the school and of the building itself, as well as of general topics such as education and architecture in the region and the occupation of New Bern by Federal troops during the Civil War. The goal of the

America's Four Hundredth Anniversary Committee: Commemoration of the Roanoke Voyages

The Museum of History's 1985 exhibit *Raleigh and Roanoke* was timed to coincide with the 400th anniversary of the Roanoke voyages. This display case highlighted pieces on loan from the armories of the Tower of London.

In the 1980s, North Carolina held a multifaceted celebration to mark the four hundredth anniversary of the first English efforts to colonize the New World. The attempts by the English, carried out between 1584 and 1587, became known as the Roanoke Voyages. In 1955 Lindsay C. Warren, a resident of the Outer Banks and a former congressman, proposed "a national or even a world's fair or exposition" in 1985 to commemorate the English landing at Roanoke Island in 1585. In 1956 legislators passed a resolution that called on the governor to appoint an America's Four Hundredth Anniversary Commission, but Gov. Luther H. Hodges never appointed members to that board.

In 1973 the General Assembly repealed the 1955 resolution and created America's Four Hundredth Anniversary Committee (AFHAC). The committee's charge was to advise the secretary of Cultural Resources on such a commemoration. Gov. James B. Hunt Jr. appointed members to AFHAC in 1978. A number of prominent North Carolinians served on the committee over the years, perhaps the best known being playwright Paul Green and actor Andy Griffith. The American Quadricentennial Corporation, a nonprofit support organization, raised private funds for the four-hundredth anniversary commemoration. AFHAC attempted to create local committees in every county. Quadricentennial celebrations took place throughout the state. In Rutherford County, reenactments of American Indian and Elizabethan culture took place as part of a "First Colonie Faire" and, in Surry County, regional history was tied to the celebration of the Great Wagon Road.

The first of the sanctioned events took place in April 1984 in Plymouth, England; it commemorated the departure of the expedition led by Philip Amadas and Arthur Barlowe. In July 1984 Princess Anne, daughter of Queen Elizabeth II, participated in an event at

interpretations at the academy building, which opened to the public in December 1990, was to place the rest of the restoration complex in historical context. Because of increasing visitation in the mid-1980s, Tryon Palace began opening on Mondays, previously the one day that operations were closed to the public.

The Archives and Records Section benefited from a needs/assessment study conducted by the National Historical Publications and Records Commission, begun in 1982 and completed in 1983. The study, part of a nationwide survey of archival programs, focused on seven archival agencies and included a planning session, public hearings, and extensive questionnaire-based research, with results compiled into a draft report published in June 1983. Among the major points targeted for attention or improvement: lack of storage space, obsolete and inadequate equipment, numerous state agencies unaware of sound records-management practices, and too many state agency records in need of arrangement and description. The study also recommended creation of a statewide archival association to bring together professionals in the field. The Society of North Carolina Archivists, officially formed in March 1983, was an outgrowth of the recommendation. In a neighborly show of goodwill, North Carolina loaned the 1663

Roanoke Island recalling the landing of that expedition. Other commemorations honored the Ralph Lane and John White colonies. The final observances took place in August 1987 to mark the anniversaries of Manteo's baptism and Virginia Dare's birth.

The Department of Cultural Resources in June 1984 sponsored the British American Festival at Duke University. In 1985 an exhibition titled *Raleigh & Roanoke* premiered at the North Carolina Museum of History after first opening at the British Library in London. The first international exhibition for the museum included Elizabethan-era items, among them original John White drawings. A scholarly conference coincided with the exhibit opening. The *Elizabeth II,* replica of a vessel used by the colonists, was constructed in Manteo and launched in 1983. The ship visited several locales along the North Carolina coast during the quadricentennial. Presently the ship is an integral attraction at the Roanoke Island Festival Park in Manteo. Archaeologists searched for the "Cittie of Raleigh" but focused more effort on researching Algonquian Indian culture. The AFHAC, in cooperation with Archives and

The *Elizabeth II,* a replica of the ship used by the Roanoke colonists, was launched at Manteo in November 1983. The ship was constructed to commemorate the 400th anniversary of the English landing at Roanoke Island in 1584.

History's Historical Publications Section, issued a number of books and pamphlets for both scholarly and general audiences during the commemoration. Brochure sets were donated to schools and libraries. The cornerstone of the quadricentennial publications program, according to the final committee report, was the new edition of the John White drawings.— *Dennis F. Daniels*

Carolina Charter to South Carolina for that state's bicentennial celebration. A special police escort traveled with the priceless document to the Palmetto State, where it was displayed from December 1982 to February 1983.

Two projects conducted by the Archives and Records Section that peaked during the 1980s involved a massive compilation of data. Biographical information about every one of the state's legislators was a carryover project from the days when the Legislative Reference Department was under the purview of the Historical Commission. The accumulation of data about abandoned cemeteries continued the work begun by the WPA. It eventually evolved into a statewide volunteer effort to record data about every cemetery by county.

In commemoration of Memorial Day in 1987, the North Carolina Vietnam Veterans Memorial Statue was dedicated on the Capitol grounds. Abbe Godwin, a North Carolinian, sculpted the realistic portrayal of combat troops, titled *After the Firefight.* The artwork, placed on the northeast grounds of the property, was the first monument erected on Union (Capitol) Square since 1948. Also in the mid-1980s, existing statuary had been restored with the aid of a grant in the

The Vietnam Veterans Memorial statue titled *After the Firefight* was sculpted by North Carolinian Abbe Godwin. The statue, dedicated on Memorial Day 1987, now stands on the northeast grounds of Union (Capitol) Square.

amount of $40,000 from the Woman's Club of Raleigh and additional money donated by concerned citizens. The Raleigh Host Lions Club assisted the Capital Area Visitor Center in achieving its goal of creating a picnic area near the state-government complex. The Lions Club donated $1,800 for picnic tables and landscaping materials for the area, which was dedicated in June 1984. The Visitor Center saw increased traffic during the late 1980s and eventually acquired a computer to help with scheduling tours.

Over the course of the first six months of 1987, William S. Price Jr., director of the Division of Archives and History, offered section administrators the opportunity to take a thirty- to sixty-day research sabbatical. The stipulation was that the individuals should select for their sabbaticals topics of division-wide scope or of a historical nature, presented in such a way as to highlight the division and its mission. Participating section administrators prepared written reports at the conclusion of their respective research projects. Branch heads gained the opportunity to serve as section administrators during the sabbaticals. A year after the conclusion of the experiment, Price regarded the sabbaticals as successful, having "unleashed an extraordinary amount of thoughtful, useful work." Under such competent leadership on many levels, the division approached its ninth decade of public service.

10

The Nineties and Beyond: Casting a Wide Net

The agency's use of computerization in the 1980s was soon eclipsed by its accomplishments in the 1990s and beyond. Most notable was the development of an agency Internet presence. The first World Wide Web page, one for the State Public Records Cataloging Services group (SPRCS), providing guidelines for managing electronic records, was launched in late 1995. Shortly thereafter it was expanded with the addition of links to the Survey and Planning Branch, the Archives and Records Section, and the Archaeology Branch. The division established a Web committee to act as an adjunct to the public relations arm of the agency. It was anticipated that the Internet would offer a means of disseminating information about all levels of Archives and History activity, and plans were made to include every unit. Overall the Internet has helped to make the public increasingly aware of the agency's mission, with the Historical Publications and Historic Sites Sections likely benefiting most directly. During the spring of 1997 the Museum of History launched a World Wide Web page that provided information about exhibits and programs and offered an opportunity to schedule visits electronically. By 1999 electronic teacher workshops were offered regularly, and the museum's Information Highway site, which employs two-way video teleconferencing, had entered classrooms throughout the state.

The Archives and Records Section's Internet presence brought mixed results. While the public has been provided with helpful information about the records the section holds and the services it offers, the number of inquiries received via the Internet has increased steadily; moreover, the inquiries themselves tend to be more demanding, both in frequency and in expectation, than do postal inquiries. The State Archives' computerized finding aid system, MARS, was made available via the Internet in December 1998, after having been taken off-line for several years because of problems involving security of digital records and the overloading of the system resulting from extremely heavy usage. Additions to and minor revisions of the division's Web page have been frequent over the years, and a major renovation occurred in June 2000. This aspect of the chronicles of Archives and History continues to be written.

NORTH CAROLINA
OFFICE *of* ARCHIVES
and HISTORY

Monday, December 2, 2002
Welcome to the North Carolina Office of Archives and History

Public History Services

- Visits and Tours
- Education and Outreach
- North Carolina Museum of History
- Historical Publications
- State Archives
- State Historical Records Advisory Board
- Government Records
- Office of State Archaeology
- Historic Preservation
- Affiliate Organizations
- Office of Archives & History Organization and Staff

FEATURES

- **Calendar/News**
- **Services Index**
- **SEARCH ►**
- **Contact Us**
- **N.C. Historical Commission**

A Service of the
North Carolina
Department of
Cultural Resources

Queen Anne's Revenge
Blackbeard

The division's web site, a portion of which is represented here, is the most technologically advanced way for researchers to make inquiries. The number of requests via the Internet has steadily increased in recent years as researchers use this new tool for research. The address of the web site is *www.ah.dcr.state.nc.us.*

A number of anniversary events were commemorated during the decade, the most extensive being the 125th anniversary of the end of the Civil War. The Historic Sites Section hosted many related activities during 1990, including a reenactment of the surrender at Bennett Place, a nighttime re-creation of the surrender of Fort Fisher with re-enactors from Massachusetts portraying the Twenty-seventh U.S. Colored Infantry, and a massive gathering at the reenactment of the Battle of Bentonville. With nearly 35,000 spectators and 2,300 participants over the course of the three-day event, it likely was the largest living history event ever held in North Carolina. That same year, Bentonville Battleground co-hosted with East Carolina University's Division of Continuing Education a national seminar on Civil War medicine. As a result of the popularity of the Bentonville events, the site began a continuing land acquisition program with the aid of the National Association for the Preservation of Civil War Sites, which purchased and donated more than seven acres adjacent to the site. Commemorating the end of the Civil War, from April to June the Capitol hosted a living history program in which six Raleigh actors portrayed characters who related their experiences in Raleigh during the spring of 1865. There was also a re-creation of the last signal message sent from the State Capitol roof by the United States Army Signal Corps, with specially made reproduction rockets repeating the original message, "Peace on Earth, good will to men."

For the State Capitol, 1990 marked the 150th anniversary of the completion of the building. Special programs included a "Feast for Five Hundred," held on the Capitol grounds on June 10 to commemorate the original dedication of the building. The Fourth of July parade that year, the first sponsored by the State Capitol Foundation, was televised live, with approximately twenty thousand spectators in attendance. On Memorial Day a veterans monument, honoring veterans of World Wars I and II and the Korean War, was dedicated. The driveway on the north side of Capitol Square had to be relocated to accommodate the commanding memorial. The following year, the staff of the Capital Area Visitor Center helped with the production of a centennial history of the Executive Mansion and with special events surrounding the celebration of that anniversary. Throughout the 1990s extensive paint research was conducted, and 1840 decorative paint effects were re-created. Toward the end of the decade, the Capitol was rewired, the exterior was repainted, and exterior lighting was renovated. For the Capitol's 160th anniversary in June 2000, the celebration was as much for the completion of the restoration as for the milestone year. A special joint session of the legislature met in the restored chambers, and a series of lectures took place on-site.

In May 1996 the Alamance Battleground site commemorated the 225th anniversary of the Battle of Alamance. The event featured the first official reenactment of the two-hour battle and a presentation of a historical drama titled *Loyal Revolt*, which focused on the Regulators and life in colonial North Carolina. In 1999 Reed Gold Mine celebrated the bicentennial of the discovery of gold at the site. The division issued two new publications—a new history of Reed and a new volume on gold and gold mining in general and within North Carolina in particular. Reed produced a new play titled *Come Forth as Gold* and presented it both at the site and at other local venues. In August 2001, in commemoration of the 220th anniversary of the Revolutionary War skirmish at the House in the Horseshoe, the site hosted the first reenactment staged on all four sides of the house. The event required careful crowd control, with 285 volunteers, staff, and reenactors participating. In September 2000, during the four-month-long celebration of the one hundredth anniversary of Thomas Wolfe's birth, the U.S. Postal Service issued a 33-cent commemorative postage stamp and officially unveiled it at the memorial in Asheville. In January 2001, for the centennial of Charles B. Aycock's inauguration as governor, the birthplace staff, Wayne County Community College, and the North Carolina Humanities Council cosponsored a symposium dealing with education, politics, and race relations in the Progressive Era.

In sharp contrast to the festive anniversary celebrations, the 1990s also brought disasters. A failure of the heating, ventilation, and air-conditioning system in the stacks of the State Archives in April 1995 caused temperatures to soar to 80 degrees, resulting in a serious outbreak of mold. Temporary staff was hired to assist with a "mold patrol" in the stacks to locate outbreaks of this threat to the records. The temporaries, led by senior staff, conducted systematic searches in the county records in the areas known to have mold susceptibility. Two noteworthy fires occurred at state historic sites during the 1990s. In July 1993 vandals damaged the Burial House at Town Creek Indian Mound, deliberately setting it afire. Although volunteer firefighters expeditiously extinguished the fire, the roof and an exhibit inside were destroyed. A restored Burial House, with a new

In July 1998 an arsonist set fire to the boardinghouse at the Thomas Wolfe Memorial causing an estimated $2.2 million in damage. About one quarter of the interior rooms were substantially affected by the fire, and the entire house sustained smoke and water damage. The photograph on the right shows the devastation in the room occupied by Thomas Wolfe's brother Ben, whose death in this room provided the basis for one of the most emotional scenes of the novel *Look Homeward, Angel*.

audiovisual display, was dedicated in 1997. In July 1998 an arsonist set fire to the boardinghouse at the Thomas Wolfe Memorial, causing an estimated $2.2 million in damage. Many rooms and furnishings were destroyed, but some recovered artifacts were fit to restore. The boardinghouse is being rebuilt at present.

In the late 1990s hurricanes took a toll on the state's historic sites. In 1999 Hurricane Floyd caused extensive flooding throughout the eastern part of the state. Archives and Records Section staff members Becky McGee-Lankford and David Mitchell (*right*) provided assistance with the recovery of records in the Princeville town hall. In March 2000, staff members from the Historic Preservation Office conducted a survey of the flood-ravaged town of Princeville. Pictured (*above*) from left to right, are: Paul Biers, Federal Emergency Management Administration consultant; and HPO preservation specialists Jennifer Martin, Catherine Bishir, and Beth Keane.

Chapter Ten

Three major hurricanes affected the agency in the 1990s—Bertha (July 1996), Fran (September 1996), and Floyd (September 1999). Historic sites sustained damage from each storm. Hurricane Fran produced rainfall that caused the Neuse River to flood the CSS *Neuse* hull with fifteen inches of water. Following that calamity, the gunboat was moved to higher ground, out of the floodplain, in 1998. Hurricane Fran ransacked the Raleigh area, and among other damage produced flooding that affected the State Archives' Old State Farmer's Market off-site storage facility. Many of the records housed there were damaged by floodwaters and mold. A commercial recovery firm was hired to deal with the affected records of archival value. Fran also wreaked havoc on historic properties, causing an 85 percent increase in technical and advisory services rendered by the State Historic Preservation Office (HPO). Fifty-eight counties incurred more than four billion dollars' worth of damages as a result of Fran.

With the memory of Fran still fresh, Hurricane Floyd roared into the state in September 1999. The hardest-hit among the historic sites was the CSS *Neuse* visitor center, left under three feet of floodwater. Fortunately, the precautions taken with the gunboat after Fran kept the river from reclaiming its namesake. Fort Fisher was closed for five months because of damage incurred from Floyd. Records and historic properties in many counties and municipalities were affected, resulting in another increase in outreach in the form of consultations on disaster planning, preparedness, salvage, and recovery. Once again, thanks to lessons learned from Hurricane Fran, the Survey and Planning Branch of the HPO was able to rush disaster-response information to owners of National Register properties and to local governments, and the Archives and Records Section provided much-needed preservation assistance. The division's budget suffered for years as a result of relief projects related to Floyd and, to a lesser extent, Fran. Support organizations played a crucial role in helping sites and other branches accomplish their missions in the wake of the hurricanes of the nineties.

Maritime history has always captured North Carolinians' imagination, but never so much as in the 1990s and beyond. In November 1991 the Underwater Archaeology Unit (UAU) dedicated the first state-designated historic shipwreck preserve, the USS *Huron* at Nags Head, for the purpose of promoting recreational diving, historical interpretation, and preservation. A grant from the Outer Banks Community Foundation made possible the construction of a gazebo to accompany the exhibit, an interpretive brochure, and a traveling display. The UAU capitalized on the growing interest in maritime history by collaborating with Wilmington's Cape Fear Museum on an educational outreach program in September 1994. The program titled "Hidden Beneath the Waves" consisted of a kit including a video, replica artifacts, research exercises, quiz games, and a four-foot model of a wreck on the bottom of the Cape Fear River.

Queen Anne's Revenge: *The Wreck of Blackbeard's Flagship?*

In June 1718 a large, heavily armed pirate ship ran aground in North Carolina waters off Topsail (now Beaufort) Inlet, setting the stage for one of history's enduring mysteries. The vessel was the *Queen Anne's Revenge* (*QAR*); its captain, the fearsome Blackbeard (Edward Thatch, or Teach), met a bloody end five months later at the hands of the Royal Navy. The *QAR*, once the flagship of a marauding pirate fleet, was left to break apart. As time passed, the facts of Blackbeard's life became the province of legend, and the wreck's location was lost to history.

In 1996, following a decade of research and unrewarding fieldwork near Beaufort Inlet, employees of Intersal, Inc., a professional maritime salvaging firm, honed in on a conglomeration of large cannons and anchors less than thirty feet below the surface. The location, position, and age of the wreckage, as well as the type of armament that accompanied it, suggested a single candidate. A press conference in Raleigh on March 3, 1997, announced the news with the cautionary note that definitive proof remained to be discovered. The site is now under the jurisdiction of the state of North Carolina, in partnership with Intersal. The site of the oldest known shipwreck in North Carolina waters through its presumed association with Blackbeard is one of the most important discoveries in the history of nautical archaeology. The debris field is protected by a strict security zone, monitored by electronic surveillance equipment linked via computer to local law enforcement officials. The Office of Archives and History presides over the excavation and preservation of the wreck through its Underwater Archaeology Unit at Kure Beach and the North Carolina Maritime Museum at Beaufort. In a cooperative venture, the remains have been under intensive investigation since 1996 with assistance from East Carolina University and other institutions.

Funding for the project has been a challenge from the outset. The General Assembly provided initial funds (supplemented by additional public and private donations), but by 2000 budget constraints threatened to curtail research efforts. In December 2001, the project received a welcome boost with a $350,000 grant from the National Endowment of the Arts. The "Save America's Treasures" funds are currrently being applied toward conservation and storage of approximately ten thousand artifacts recovered from the wreck. In the fall of 2001, educational outreach included the popular "*QAR* DiveLive," during which students were treated to live Internet broadcasts from the wreck site. Video feeds included underwater tours of the ship's remains, tours of the conservation lab, and

---

The activities taught students about contemporary problems experienced by archaeologists.

The March 1997 announcement of the discovery of what archaeologists believed to be the remains of Blackbeard's flagship *Queen Anne's Revenge* (*QAR*) brought unprecedented public attention to Archives and History, the underwater archaeology program, and North Carolina's maritime history in general. Partly because of that discovery, the Archaeology Branch became an autonomous section in 2001. Hour-long documentaries by the British Broadcasting Corporation and the North Carolina Center for Public Television and an article in *Smithsonian* magazine were among the highlights of the early publicity. The North Carolina Maritime Museum at Beaufort, designated as the facility to curate the artifacts collected from the *QAR* project, was transferred from the Department of Agriculture and Consumer Services to the Division of Archives

interactive project updates. Public interest remains high as project officials share their findings.

Is this really Blackbeard's flagship? Will a definitive discovery emerge to erase all doubt? Perhaps not, but the evidence speaks volumes. What archaeologists presume to be the *QAR* offers tantalizing clues to eighteenth-century maritime activity in the Americas. With each new discovery, scientists and historians gain valuable insight in areas such as naval armament, ship construction, colonial provisioning, and seafaring life. The shipwreck, lost for nearly three centuries, offers a tangible link to the Golden Age of Piracy—a romanticized era long obscured by myth and legend.—*Mark Anderson Moore*

A press conference was held in March 1997 to announce the discovery of what researchers believed to be Blackbeard's flagship *Queen Anne's Revenge*. From left to right: Mike Daniel and Phil Masters, of Intersal, Inc.; Richard Lawrence, Underwater Archaeology Unit; Steve Claggett, State Archaeologist; Wilson Angley and Jerry C. Cashion, Research Branch; and Jeffrey J. Crow, director, Archives and History. The ship is a model of what the *QAR* is thought to have looked like. A recovered blunderbuss barrel and a blunderbuss are visible on the table to the right.

and History in October 1997. The following year the Maritime Museum acquired artifacts from the defunct Barbour Boat Works of New Bern, the last operating major shipyard in North Carolina. Salvage and conservation of the Barbour artifacts and records was a joint operation involving staff members from the Maritime Museum, the East Carolina University Manuscript Collection, and Tryon Palace. The state purchased the six-acre shipyard tract for development as a history education and visitor center for Tryon Palace Historic Sites & Gardens. Not only did the addition of the Maritime Museum provide a home for the *QAR* project materials but it also diversified the educational outreach of the entire division. The museum offers educational programs in the natural sciences and public programs on watercraft building. Since the Harvey W. Smith Watercraft Center began offering classes to the public in 1993, the museum's programs have drawn people from throughout the nation. The Maritime

Western Office staff archaeologists were involved in the construction of a reproduction sixteenth-century Cherokee house at the Museum of the Cherokee Indian in Cherokee in 1993. The structure serves as an outdoor exhibit at the museum.

Museum also serves as an outpost for youth activities such as regional historical events. In 1998 the Maritime Museum expanded, acquiring the Maritime Museum at Southport as a branch. In 1999 Archives and History further expanded its maritime history presence by creating a third maritime museum branch at Roanoke Island.

The Western Office of Archives and History in September 1991 vacated offices in Oteen when Western Carolina University, the landlord, elected to dispose of the facility for financial reasons. At that time, Western Office staff members moved to temporary quarters in Arden, paying higher rent for less space. In December the Arden facility was burglarized and about four thousand dollars' worth of equipment was stolen and never recovered. Two years later the Western Office moved into the Clarence Barker House, a National Register property in Asheville's Biltmore Village.

During the early 1990s the Western Office established a historic preservation internship through the public history program at Middle Tennessee State University, Murfreesboro. The Western Office staff helped to plan and implement a historic preservation workshop with the Carl Sandburg National Historic Site in Flat Rock. During the 1992-1994 biennium, David Moore, the Western Office archaeologist, assisted the Museum of the Cherokee Indian in the construction of a replica sixteenth-century Cherokee village. Serving a growing audience, the

Approximately 25,000 people attended the two-day festival celebrating the opening of the new Museum of History on April 23-24, 1994 (*left*). The lobby of the new facility displays a reproduction of the Wright Brothers flier (*below*).

Mountain Gateway Museum in Old Fort opened an amphitheater in April 1993. The facility's creek-side location and distinctive stone architecture made it popular for community activities and museum functions. In 1994 the Mountain Gateway Museum entered into an exhibit exchange with Brunnenburg Agriculture Museum in Dorf Tirol, Italy. The two museums, whose interpretive activities bore marked similarities, exchanged regional photographs and documents for four years and continue to remain in close contact. In 1999 the Museum of the Albemarle hosted a groundbreaking for a new 50,000-square-foot museum building located in downtown Elizabeth City and overlooking the Pasquotank River. The Friends of the Museum of the Albemarle, the museum's support group, raised more than $1.5 million to construct exhibits for the new facility.

The North Carolina Museum of History began moving staff members into its new but unfinished facility in August 1992. The museum's opening in April 1994 marked the first time in many years that its entire staff was housed under one roof. Opening ceremonies included a "Parade of Transportation," music, dancing, and storytelling, as well as an evening panel discussion that featured the participation of all the state's living governors. Premiering along with the building was the award-winning *North Carolina Women Making History*, an exhibit that required ten years of research and planning. The new facility's exhibit space tripled that of the old location in the Archives and History/State Library Building. The increased space allowed for improved educational programming, including frequently scheduled special tours, a Gallery Theater, musical performances, demonstrations, summer camps, scholarly symposia, and workshops. One of the more notable exhibits to open in the new building, *Health and Healing Experiences in North Carolina* (1998), received both regional and national awards. Effective February 1, 1996, the Museum of History separated from the Division of Archives and History to become an autonomous division. That arrangement continued until a widely ranging reorganization took place in 2001.

The Archives and Records Section was involved in numerous outreach programs in the 1990s. Perhaps the most significant project was the collaborative effort made possible by a grant in excess of fifty thousand dollars received from the National Historical Publications and Records Commission (NHPRC) in July 1992. With those funds the staff created standard computer descriptions of state agency records for submission to national databases and for an in-house database. The staff likewise produced a *Guide to Research Materials in the North Carolina State Archives: State Agency Records*, published in 1995. The comprehensive volume included histories of state agencies and descriptions of archival-quality agency records held both in the Archives and the State Records Center. Later in 1995 the Research Libraries Group selected the State Archives to participate in what became known as "Marriage, Women, and the Law, 1815-1914," a digitization project focusing on marriage law. At the close of the project in 1998, nine thousand images had been filmed and digitized by a commercial vendor, then described and prepared for posting on the World Wide Web. The following year, the State Historical Records Advisory Board utilized an NHPRC grant to fund a series of educational teleconferences designed to bring together archivists from throughout the state to share ideas and discuss issues.

Reminiscent of the Historical Commission's early goals, the Archives and Records Section in July 1996 formed the Military Collection Project to gather information and further document North Carolina's role in twentieth-century wars. The project began with an effort to document World War I, especially through first-person interviews and photographs still in private hands. With participation from citizens statewide, the military project has obtained materials representing about sixteen hundred of North Carolina's soldiers and each twentieth-century conflict.

In 1998 the legislature provided funds enabling the Archives and Records Section to lease approximately 20,000 square feet of warehouse space for storage of noncurrent state agency records. Use of the Blount Street Annex, as the warehouse was named, was to be a provisional measure. The objective was not to serve long-term space needs, since use of the annex decreased efficiency and increased service time, making staff responsible for servicing records off-site; and while the annex has an independent heating, ventilation, and air-conditioning system, it did not meet the stringent criteria necessary for the storage of nontextual materials. The annex offered the Records Center storage space for 66,000 cubic feet of records. The additional space enabled state agencies to transfer records without delay (and in accordance with their official records-retention schedules) for the first time in years.

In 1990 the Historical Publications Section closed the biennium with markedly increased sales, breaking previous annual and biennial records. The North Carolina Literary and Historical Association hosted a celebratory reception at the State Capitol for the Publications staff. By that time the section was typesetting some of its publications in-house, producing savings of 40 percent and speeding up the production of galley proofs. With the January 1992 issue of the *North Carolina Historical Review,* the section implemented new desktop publishing procedures, which not only improved the appearance of the periodical but also saved a considerable amount of money. In 2000 the Historical Publications Section published the third volume of governors' papers for James Baxter Hunt Jr. The mandated publication of the chief executive's official records has been ongoing since publication of the papers of Thomas Walter Bickett in 1923. In July 1999 the section began accepting credit-card payments for the first time, expediting orders and boosting sales. Beginning in 2001 nearly all new titles were typeset in-house, making use of new technology.

Former governor James B. Hunt Jr. signs a copy of *Addresses and Public Papers of James Baxter Hunt Jr., Governor of North Carolina,* Volume III, *1993-1997* for Jan-Michael Poff (*right*), editor of this and three previous volumes of governors' papers.

During the 1990-1992 biennium, what was then the Technical Services Branch of the Archives and Records Section received a grant in the amount of $588,163 from the National Endowment for the Humanities to enable the State Archives and the State Library to catalog all North Carolina-based newspapers held in repositories throughout the state and to locate issues of North Carolina newspapers previously not identified. After forty years of work, with and without grants, the North Carolina Newspaper Project completed its portion of the United States Newspaper Program in 1998. More than three million newspaper pages were microfilmed, with newspapers identified for ninety-nine of North Carolina's one hundred counties.

The December 1990 publication of *North Carolina Architecture,* by Catherine W. Bishir of the Survey and Planning Branch of the Archaeology and Historic Preservation Section, culminated twenty years of work by the author. The

Historic Preservation Foundation of North Carolina sponsored the project to commemorate the 1939 founding of its predecessor organization, the North Carolina Society for the Preservation of Antiquities (NCSPA). Survey and Planning staff assisted with the production of the volume by rearranging positions and duties to accommodate Bishir's work on the project. Whereas earlier surveys had tended to focus exclusively on grandiose examples, *North Carolina Architecture* reflected on both the modest and the grand. The book won national attention as a model for state architectural surveys.

In the mid-1990s the State Historic Preservation Office (HPO) increased its public education programs through the distribution of a variety of literature: a bimonthly newsletter for local preservation commissions; *The Handbook for Historic Preservation Commissions*, published in 1994 in conjunction with the present incarnation of the NCSPA, Preservation North Carolina; county fact sheets detailing preservation activities at the county level; and a *Guide to the Historic Architecture of Eastern North Carolina* (1996), the first of three proposed regional volumes (with the *Guide to the Historic Architecture of Western North Carolina* following in 1999). As a result of that public outreach, during the 1994-1996 biennium, Survey and Planning experienced a 98.6 percent increase in the number of field visits to historic properties and a corresponding increase in the number of public requests and consultations. At the same time, the division's Eastern Office, administered by the HPO, saw an increased number of site visits.

On January 12, 1998, deputy state historic preservation officer David Brook (*seated*) officially approved plans submitted as part of the first State Historic Rehabilitation Tax Credit Application for Non-Income Producing Historic Structures. Standing behind Brook are (*left to right*) A. L. Honeycutt Jr., Claudia R. Brown, Tim E. Simmons, and Robin J. Stancil.

During the 1994-1996 biennium, the HPO, following five years of staff work and citizen involvement, published *Legacy: A Preservation Guide into the Twenty-First Century*. The booklet, approved by the North Carolina Historical Commission and the National Park Service, laid out a comprehensive preservation plan for the state. The 1997 legislature provided for a 30 percent income tax credit for the rehabilitation of non-income-producing properties, which went into effect January 1998. It likewise increased the credit for income-producing properties from 5 to 20 percent. The HPO's Restoration Branch staff drafted administrative rules, design guidelines, applications, and instructions for the program. Staff led workshops and gave presentations on the new tax credits to students at the North Carolina State University School of Design, to citizens groups throughout the state, and at preservation conferences.

Supported by the HPO, the North Carolina African American Network on Historic Preservation was established in March 1998 following almost two years of planning by a twenty-five-member task force. The network is a membership organization with the primary goals of education, enhancement of economic development, and support of preservation groups in African American communities. During the group's first year, regional meetings were held in Asheville, Wilmington, and Concord, giving citizens the chance to share information about historic preservation projects, opportunities, and challenges in African American communities.

In the mid-1990s the HPO's Archaeology Branch, with the aid of the North Carolina Department of Transportation, secured special federal funds to develop a research center. Selected as the site was the former textbook warehouse on Lane Street in Raleigh. The 14,400-square-foot facility, completed in November 1998, includes an archives, two laboratories, a conservation treatment area, a records repository, a photographic studio, and a darkroom. There the branch staff is able to provide occasional technical and professional assistance to law enforcement agencies; the center also serves as an adjunct educational laboratory for undergraduate and graduate students. The building houses more than two million artifacts and is the first facility specifically dedicated to archival preservation of the state's collections. The Research Center provides access to the state's archaeological heritage through organized collections, computer databases, digital images, displays, publications, and Internet sites.

Renovations to the State Capitol during the early to mid-1990s, particularly an extensive interior paint restoration, led to an intriguing discovery. A small account book, a personal letter, and an 1863 Valentine poem were found atop the shelving in the State Geologist's Office. Those items are likely the only Civil War-era materials successfully hidden in the Capitol during the 1865 Federal occupation. Tryon Palace researchers experienced their own extraordinary find in the early 1990s: a four-page manuscript description of the palace gardens in 1783, complete with a map depicting the layout. The materials were discovered in a Venezuelan archives in the papers of diplomat Francisco de Miranda, who had obtained them directly from architect John Hawks. Palace staff studied the papers and used them in interpreting the palace garden.

During the 1992-1994 biennium Tryon Palace initiated several new educational programs, including the Behind the Scenes tour, which highlights the research and interpretations behind displays, and the "Young Sprouts" garden education program, targeted at second-graders to teach practical applications of math and science skills. Palace staff devoted increased attention to Civil War interpretations, beginning with Union Occupation Days, an event featuring various activities, including an interpreter who portrayed a member of the 44th Massachusetts Volunteers, a Union army unit stationed in Federally occupied New Bern. Civil War interpretations increased in direct response to the popularity of the theme. At Christmastime the palace's Civil War interpreters devoted one week to portraying Confederate soldiers and one week to portraying Union personnel. Activities for children, including workshops on specific crafts or events, as well as the full week-long History Day Camp, were expanded. By the end of the 1990s, plans to begin a project aimed at researching, documenting, and publicizing the history of African Americans in the New Bern area were coming to fruition. Community involvement and public awareness were primary goals.

The much-anticipated Douglas Preservation Center opened at Tryon Palace during the latter part of the decade, offering a central location for carpentry, paint, and maintenance, as well as storage space for artifacts and documents. The scripted interpretive performance *Away to Alamance* was replaced in 1998 in favor of a series of improvisational interactions. The living history exhibitions offered glimpses at all walks of life, including those of household slaves in 1770 and 1835. Offering a different representation of colonial New Bern, the Hay House opened to the public in November 1998. The home was furnished entirely in reproduction furniture crafted with authentic tools and materials that would have been available in 1830, so that interpreters and visitors alike could touch and use the furniture, thus adding to the overall experience. The Hay House offered no modern heating or cooling system, to add further to the realism.

Historic sites were updated and improved during the 1990s. Brunswick Town and House in the Horseshoe added informational wayside exhibits (built in the absence of a permanent visitor center); Fort Fisher and Bentonville Battleground each underwent major renovations to their visitor centers. In 1994 Pettigrew State Park transferred the reconstructed overseer's house at Somerset Place to the Historic Sites Section. The accession of that building aided efforts to include in interpretations all who lived on the plantation. Also to that end, excavations were completed that same year on seven structures situated in the plantation's slave community complex or grouping of houses. In 1996 the National Park Service designated Bentonville Battleground a National Historic Landmark. Horne Creek Living Historical Farm introduced a heritage orchard in 1999. Two hundred heirloom apple trees were planted—two each of one hundred varieties. The following year another two hundred were added. The produce will be utilized at the site, while the orchard itself—the largest of its kind in the South—will be a virtual museum of specimens.

With the 1996 transfer of the 1767 Chowan County Courthouse to the state, the Iredell House State Historic Site changed its name to Historic Edenton State Historic Site. During preparations for the transfer, interestingly, it was discovered that the colonial government had owned the courthouse and that the state took possession of it after the Revolutionary War. Therefore, the state already owned the courthouse, and no deed transfer was needed. In 1996 Spencer Shops, too, changed its name to the North Carolina Transportation Museum. That year the restored Robert Julian Roundhouse opened to the public. One of the largest roundhouses ever built and one of only a few remaining, the massive building offers visitors a look at more than twenty-five restored locomotives and rail cars, as well as the repair shops. In August 1999 the North Carolina Transportation Museum hosted a "guest appearance" by an operational "Thomas the Tank Engine," a character most popular with children ages three to five, that attracted 13,000 visitors. The event, now held annually in October, draws on average 35,000 to 50,000 people for a six-day program, by far the site's largest single event held each year. People have come from as far away as California and New York just to see the little blue engine.

In 1997 the division initiated annual sponsorship of National History Day, a competition designed to encourage the study of history in schools. Students in grades six through twelve compete, either individually or in groups of two to five. Projects exploring the year's theme are presented in one of four formats, each comprising its own category for judging: video, papers, performance, or exhibits. Employees of the agency and other volunteers serve as judges in the categories, selecting winners from North Carolina to compete on the national level.

In December 2000 Archives and History learned that the Department of Public Instruction was considering the discontinuation of North Carolina history as a

For History Day in April 2002, students from J. E. Holmes Middle School in Eden participated in the Junior Performance category by staging a reenactment of the Salem Witch Trials.

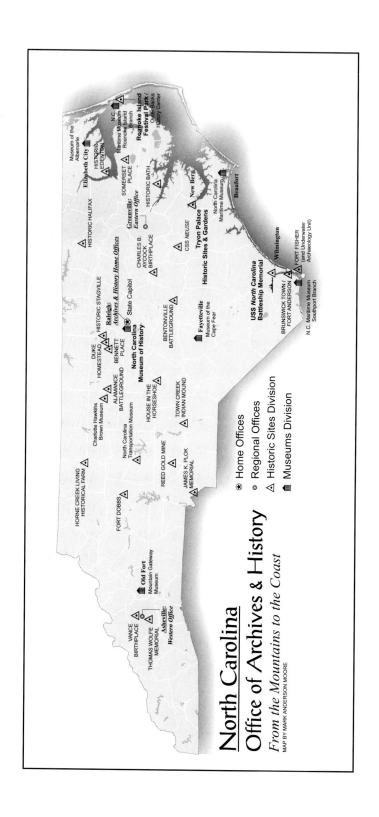

North Carolina
Office of Archives & History
From the Mountains to the Coast
MAP BY MARK ANDERSON MOORE

Home Offices

Regional Offices

Historic Sites Division

Museums Division

VANCE BIRTHPLACE

THOMAS WOLFE MEMORIAL

Asheville: *Western Office*

Old Fort Mountain Gateway Museum

HORNE CREEK LIVING HISTORICAL FARM

FORT DOBBS

Charlotte Hawkins Brown Museum

North Carolina Transportation Museum

REED GOLD MINE

JAMES K. POLK MEMORIAL

ALAMANCE BATTLEGROUND

HOUSE IN THE HORSESHOE

TOWN CREEK INDIAN MOUND

DUKE HOMESTEAD

BENNETT PLACE

HISTORIC STAGVILLE

Raleigh: *Archives & History Home Offices*

State Capitol

North Carolina Museum of History

HISTORIC HALIFAX

Museum of the Albemarle

Elizabeth City

HISTORIC EDENTON

N.C. Maritime Museum Roanoke Island Branch

Roanoke Island Festival Park / Outer Banks History Center

SOMERSET PLACE

HISTORIC BATH

Greenville: *Eastern Office*

CHARLES B. AYCOCK BIRTHPLACE

New Bern

CSS NEUSE

Tryon Palace **Historic Sites & Gardens**

North Carolina Maritime Museum

Beaufort

BENTONVILLE BATTLEGROUND

Fayetteville Museum of the Cape Fear

USS North Carolina Battleship Memorial

Wilmington

FORT FISHER (and Underwater Archaeology Unit)

BRUNSWICK TOWN / FORT ANDERSON

N.C. Maritime Museum Southport Branch

The current Historical Commission, shown with Secretary of Cultural Resources Lisbeth C. Evans (*front center*), are (*front row*) William S. Powell, Janet N. Norton, Millie M. Barbee, Jerry Cashion (*chair*), Jeffrey J. Crow, deputy secretary of the Office of Archives and History, Mary Hayes Holmes, (*second row*) N. J. Crawford, B. Perry Morrison Jr., Alan D. Watson, Freddie L. Parker, Max R. Williams, and H. G. Jones (not pictured are Paul D. Escott, Gail W. O'Brien, and Margaret Supplee Smith).

required course in the eighth-grade curriculum. Because the North Carolina Historical Commission was charged in 1903 with encouraging the study of North Carolina history and since Archives and History had taken action in a similar situation in the 1970s, director Jeffrey J. Crow organized a "Committee to Save North Carolina History in the Public Schools," which held an initial meeting in January 2001. With the help of editorials and letters to the editors appearing in various newspapers, as well as seven civic hearings held throughout the state, public attention was captured, and by March the matter was being discussed in the legislature. The state House of Representatives unanimously passed a bill requiring public schools to retain North Carolina history as a distinct subject. With the state senate leaning in the same direction, the State Board of Education in April voted to maintain the instruction of North Carolina history in the state's public schools. The entire episode can be viewed as a timely reaffirmation of the original mission of the Historical Commission. Moreover, the overwhelming public support for retaining the curriculum might be viewed as an endorsement of the achievements of the commission and its successors.

Effective October 1, 2001, Archives and History underwent reorganization as part of greater changes made within the North Carolina Department of Cultural Resources. The Division of Archives and History was divided into three distinct divisions under a new Office of Archives and History. The divisions— State History Museums, State Historic Sites, and Historical Resources—were designed "to promote greater efficiency, to foster better communication across sectional boundaries, and to create centers of excellence for programs with shared missions." The reorganization reflected the new Secretary of Cultural Resources Lisbeth C. Evans's vision of how the department should render public services, particularly given recent technological advancements. Jeffrey J. Crow was named deputy secretary of Archives and History, overseeing the three division directors as follows: Elizabeth F. Buford, director of State History Museums (returned once more to the Archives and History fold); Kay P. Williams, director of State Historic Sites; and David J. Olson, director of Historical Resources. The reorganization occurred at a time when the great expansion of the previous ninety-nine years had stagnated. As staff members entered the year 2002, a budget crisis as devastating as that of the Great Depression weighed heavily on the minds of the people in the Office of Archives and History.

In 1907 R. D. W. Connor wrote that "No people who are indifferent to their past need hope to make their future great." As the office that for nearly one hundred years has sought to make sure that the people of North Carolina are not "indifferent to their past," the agency celebrates its own history and hopes that the recognition of its accomplishments will make its own future great.

Sources Consulted

Principal sources of information for this text have been the agency's biennial reports dating from 1908 to 2000 and its bimonthly newsletter *Carolina Comments*, primarily from 1967 to the present. While the biennial reports provided many facts, *Carolina Comments* helped to fill in the needed details. Indispensable to the chronicling of events at the historic sites was a series of unpublished sketches edited by Richard F. Knapp. The sketches, cumulatively titled "North Carolina's State Historic Sites: A Brief History and Status Report," were compiled in 1995 and updated in 2000. They remain in the files of the Historic Sites Section. Also consulted was *Public History in North Carolina, 1903-1978: The Proceedings of the Seventy-fifth Anniversary Celebration, March 7, 1978* (1979), edited by Jeffrey J. Crow. That collection of essays remains an excellent source of information, especially for the advent of each section. R. D. W. Connor's 1907 report titled "The North Carolina Historical Commission" details the creation, organization, and mission of that body. The 1954 *North Carolina Historical Review* article by Henry S. Stroupe titled, "The North Carolina Department of Archives and History—The First Half Century," recounts that period of the agency's history.

Several speeches, articles, and books were useful for specific portions of the centennial history. *Time before History: The Archaeology of North Carolina*, by Trawick Ward and R. P. Stephen Davis Jr. (1999), addressed some questions about North Carolina's early archaeological programs and professionals. David L. S. Brook's *A Lasting Gift of Heritage: A History of the North Carolina Society for the Preservation of Antiquities, 1939-1974* (1997) provided details about the North Carolina Society for the Preservation of Antiquities and its early preservation efforts. Both for the individual essay on Tryon Palace and for the general history, Blackwell P. Robinson's *Three Decades of Devotion: The Tryon Palace Commission 1945-1975* (1978) was quite useful and thorough. David L. S. Brook's 1995 speech "Our Rightful Heritage" addressed both Tryon Palace's history and preservation concerns. Brook's article "Joye Jordan: Guardian of Tar Heel History," which appeared in the spring 1994 *North Carolina Historic Preservation Office Newsletter*, provided information about Jordan's career and the wonderful quote about her doing a "man's" job. Both Ansley Herring Wegner (for the main text) and Michael Hill (for the feature article) consulted Thomas C. Parramore's 1974 *North Carolina Historical Review* article, "Forging the Tremulous Link: The First Half-Century of the *North Carolina Historical Review*," which discussed the development and accomplishments of that periodical. Frank D. Gatton's master's thesis, titled "A History of Local Records in North Carolina 1665 to 1959" (North Carolina State University, 1977), is an excellent resource for information on the state's court records and various other county records that are now in the custody of the State Archives. Gatton clearly relates the struggles and achievements of that section's local records initiatives. David J. Olson's 1993 speech "The North Carolina State Archives and the Genealogical Society of Utah" (copy in the Research Branch) was helpful in describing the latter's role in the microfilming of local records. *The Carolina Charter of 1663* (1954), by William S. Powell, was the principal source for Ms. Wegner's writing about the acquisition of that document and was also used for Mark A. Moore's essay about the Carolina Charter Tercentenary Commission.

Aside from Knapp's historical sites sketches, various other types of unpublished materials were used. The Historical Commission/Archives and History director's correspondence from 1903 to 1972 filled in the narrative with interesting quotes and information that was not detailed in the biennial reports. Susan Trimble, a member of the staff of the Historical Publications Section, arranged a comprehensive listing of every publication issued directly by the agency. That compilation was and will be a useful tool in the files at the Historical Publications Section. Tom Vincent, a student at North Carolina State University, provided invaluable assistance in selecting photographs and writing captions. Various agency Web sites were useful in filling in details about programs and facilities. Verbal, e-mail, or photograph-related assistance was received from the following people: Raymond Beck, Eric Blevins, David Brook, Cathy Brown, Chandrea Burch, John Campbell, Stephen Claggett, Gina Fry, Bill Garrett, Donna Kelly, Richard Knapp, Dean Knight, Sarah Koonts, Jesse R. Lankford, Richard Lawrence, Steve Massengill, Alane Mills, David Mitchell, Thornton Mitchell, Catherine Morris, Larry Neal, Billy Oliver, Leon Sikes, Archie Smith, Michael Southern, Susan Trimble, Davis Waters, Alan Westmoreland, Jim Willard, Janice Williams, Kay Williams, and Jane Wolff. Lisa Bailey proofread the work and Ken Simpson prepared the index.

As with the main text, much of the information for the feature essays was taken from the agency's biennial reports and *Carolina Comments*. Agency Web pages were helpful, especially those of the State Historic Preservation Office and the Office of State Archaeology. Useful articles from the *North Carolina Historical Review* include Chalmers G. Davidson's "Three Hundred Years of Carolina History" (April 1963), Hugh Dorth's "Lest We Forget: North Carolina's Commemoration of the War Between the States" (April 1959), Norman Larson's "The Confederate Centennial: A Report" (April 1965), and William Burlie Brown's "The State Literary and Historical Association, 1900-1950" (April 1951). Mark A. Moore utilized newsletters from the North Carolina Confederate Centennial Commission dating from July 1960 to June 1965. Joffre Lanning Coe's *Town Creek Indian Mound: A Native American Legacy* (1995) provided most of the background for the feature on that site. The *American Archivist* was the source for R. D. W. Connor's "Advent of an American Archivist" (1942), Waldo G.

Leland's "R. D. W. Connor, First Archivist of the United States" (1953), and Terry Sanford's "North Carolina—Three Hundredth Birthday" (1964).

For the essay on *The Black Presence in North Carolina*, Dennis Daniels utilized, among other sources aforementioned, the project files at the Museum of History. For use in other essays, he relied upon final reports of America's Four Hundredth Anniversary Celebration and the North Carolina Newspaper Project, as well as an unpublished report to the 1983 General Assembly in reference to Spencer Shops. In his piece on the Tar Heel Junior Historian Association, Daniels received help from adviser Rebecca Lewis and referenced the association's twenty-fifth anniversary celebration program. For all of his essays, Daniels utilized *North Carolina Session Laws* and regional newspapers.

Index

A

D

Daniel, Mike: pictured, 89
Daughters of the American Revolution, 14
Davidson, Chalmers, 51
Day, Thomas, 69
Defunct college records, 53
Delgado, Adolfo, 45
Department of Administration, 65
Department of Agriculture, 9
Department of Art, Culture, and History, 57
Department of Community Colleges, 67
Department of Conservation and Development, 19, 20, 34, 50
Department of Cultural Resources, 57, 58, 100
Department of Public Instruction, 3, 13, 53-55, 97
Department of Transportation, 77, 95
Dillard, Richard Dixon, 2
Disaster recovery assistance, 86, 87
Division of Archives and History: appropriations to, 88; budget cuts affecting, 76, 100; court cases involving, 64; created in Department of Art, Culture, and History, 57; development of Internet presence by, 83, 84; divided into three divisions, 100; facilities of, 62, 78; legislation concerning, 80; N.C. Maritime Museum transferred to, 88-89; opens Eastern Office, 78; opens Western Office, 61-62; reorganization of, to create Archaeology Section in, 64, 88; reorganization of, to create State Capitol/Visitor Services and Historic Preservation Sections in, 62; reorganization of, to separate Museum of History from, 92; reorganization of, to split into three divisions, 100; research sabbaticals for administrators of, 82; and restoration of teaching of North Carolina history in eighth grade, 73, 97, 99; sponsorship of National History Day by, 97; utilization of automation by, 69, 71, 72-73, 83, 84
Division of Historic Sites: appropriations to, 35, 58, 59, 60, 61; educational activities of, 60; established, 34; interpretation of sites by, 46; legislation concerning, 34, 35, 61; reconstruction of sites by, 45; special events hosted by, 45, 46, 47, 60-61; visitor centers opened by, 46. *See also* Historic sites; Historic Sites Section
Division of Historic Sites and Museums, 50, 62
Division of Historical Resources, 100
Division of State Historic Sites, 100
Division of State History Museums, 100
Douglas Preservation Center, 96
Draper, Lyman, 49
Duke Homestead, 59
Duke Homestead Education and History Corporation, 59

E

East Carolina University, 78, 84, 88
East Carolina University Manuscript Collection, 89
Eastern Office of Archives and History, 78, 94
Edenton Mill Village, 25
Education and outreach activities: by Archaeology Branch, 65, 73-74, 77; by Archives and Records Section, 66-67, 74; with creation of Tar Heel Junior Historian Association, 40-41; by Federation of North Carolina Historical Societies, 61; at historic sites, 60, 74-75; by Historical Publications Section, 54-55; by mobile museum, 37-38, 47, 50, 70; by Museum of the Cape Fear, 79; by North Carolina Confederate Centennial Commission, 42, 47; by North Carolina Historical Commission, 5-6; by North Carolina Maritime Museum, 89; by North Carolina Museum of History, 38, 51-52, 69, 70, 83; at Stagville Preservation Center, 59; at State Capitol, 84; by State Historic Preservation Office, 94; at Town Creek Indian Mound, 21; at Tryon Palace, 95-96; by Underwater Archaeology Unit, 87; by Western Office of Archives and History, 78, 90
Education Building: additional space in, for Department of Archives and History, 37; appropriation for building of, 24; deficiencies of, 43; pictured, 25; public hearing concerning Daniel Boone homeplace in, 49; space in, for

North Carolina Historical Commission and Hall of History, 24-25

Edwards, Ted R.: pictured, 42

Elizabeth II, 74-75, 77-78, 81; pictured, 81

Ellington, John D., 62

Environmental assessment program, 64-65, 77

Episcopal Diocese of East Carolina, 36

Escott, Paul D., 99

Evans, Lisbeth C., 100; pictured, 99

Executive Board of Archives and History, 3, 27, 31, 32, 58

Executive Mansion, 85

Exhibits: by Archives and Records Section, 66-67; in Hall of History, 28-29, 41; at historic sites, 96; at North Carolina Museum of History, 68-71, 79-81, 91-92; at North Carolina Transportation Museum, 60; by Underwater Archaeology Unit, 87

F

Fayetteville Arsenal, 79

Federal Writers' Project, 18

Federation of North Carolina Historical Societies, 61

"First at Bethel, Farthest at Gettysburg and Chickamauga, and Last at Appomattox," 4

Fletcher, Inglis, 4

Foreign archives, 16, 55-56

Fort Anderson, 36, 60

Fort Branch, 64

Fort Caswell, 60

Fort Dobbs, 48

Fort Fisher: commemorative events at, 47; damage to by Hurricane Floyd, 87; designated as a National Historic Landmark, 45; development as historic site, 45; preservation laboratory at, 46, 50; reenactment of surrender of, 84; visitor center at, renovated, 96

Fort Macon, 34

Fort Raleigh, 21

Franklin, John Hope, 15, 28

Frazier, Charles, 4

Freeman, Edward: pictured, 37

Friends of the Archives, 68

Friends of the Museum of the Albemarle, 91

Fries, Adelaide L., 12, 15; pictured, 24

Frutchey, Lloyd, 20

Frutchey State Park, 20

G

Garden Club of North Carolina, 24

Gary, Emily Gilliam: pictured, 24

Genealogical research, 7, 30, 67, 74

Genealogical Society of Utah, 26, 29, 30

Gibbes, Annette, 74

Godwin, Abbe, 81, 82

Gold History Corporation, 58

Gosney, Jane Fetner, 24-25; pictured, 24

Governor's Archaeological Advisory Committee, 76

Governors' papers, 93

Graham, William A., 8

Green, Paul, 21, 80

Griffith, Andy, 80

Grimes, J. Bryan, 4

Guide to the Historic Architecture of Eastern North Carolina, A, 55, 94

Guide to the Historic Architecture of Western North Carolina, A, 55, 94

Guide to North Carolina Newspapers on Microfilm, 39

Guide to Research Materials in the North Carolina State Archives: State Agency Records, 92

Guilford Battleground National Military Park, 46

H

Haley, Alex, 67

Hall of History: becomes Museum Division, 32; collections for, by Fred A. Olds, 10; educational activities of, 37-38, 40-41; establishes Tar Heel Junior Historian Association, 38, 40; exhibits gowns of governors' wives, 28; exhibits military collection, 29; exhibits street scenes, 41; iconographic collection of, 1; inventory of collections by, 32; name changed to North Carolina Museum of History, 50; pictured, 9, 29, 41; portrait collection of, 27; space problems of, 24; storage facilities of, 7, 24-25; transferred to Historical Commission, 9, 10; during World War II, 27

Hamilton, J. G. de Roulhac, 2, 5, 14

Moore County Historical Association, 35, 59

Moore, David, 90

Moore, Marie D., 15

Moravian records, 12, 18

Morris, Catherine J.: pictured, 73

Morris, Richard, 18

Morrison, B. Perry, Jr.: pictured, 99

Mountain Gateway Museum, 78, 90-91

Murray, D. C., 47

Museum of the Albemarle, 62, 74, 91

Museum of the Cape Fear, 78-79

Museum of the Cherokee Indian, 90

Museum of History. *See* North Carolina Museum of History

Museum of History Associates, 40, 68

Museum of Natural Sciences, 9

N

National Association for the Preservation of Civil War Sites, 84

National Endowment of the Arts, 88

National Endowment for the Humanities: provides funding for *The Black Presence in North Carolina* exhibit, 69, 70; provides funding to Carolina Charter Corporation, 51; provides funding for newspaper surveys, 39, 93; provides funding for publication of *The Way We Lived in North Carolina*, 74

National Historic Landmarks, 21, 45, 58, 96

National Historic Preservation Act of 1966, 56

National Historical Publications and Records Commission, 80, 92

National History Day, 97

National Oceanic and Atmospheric Administration, 65

National Register of Historic Places, 54-55, 56, 64

New Bern Academy, 79-80

New Bern Public Library, 56

New River basin, 64-65

Newsome, Albert Ray, 12-13, 14, 17, 23

Newspaper Microfilm Project, 39

Noble, M. C. S., 15

North Carolina African American Network on Historic Preservation, 95

North Carolina American Revolution Bicentennial Commission, 57

North Carolina Archaeological Council, 76

North Carolina Archaeological Society, 5

North Carolina Architecture, 93-94

North Carolina Art Society, 5

North Carolina Booklet, 14

North Carolina Confederate Centennial Commission, 42, 46, 47, 55

North Carolina Coordinating Committee for the Advancement of History, 41

North Carolina Day, 5

North Carolina Folklore Society, 4-5

North Carolina: A Guide to the Old North State, 18

North Carolina Higher-Court Records, 1709-1723, 66

North Carolina Highway Historical Marker Advisory Committee, 19

North Carolina Historical Commission: appropriations to, for historical markers, 8, 19; appropriations to, for operating budget, 2, 17, 21; appropriations to, for war records program, 28; archaeology program of, 20; archival program of, 3, 4, 9, 18, 23; becomes Executive Board of Archives and History, 27, 58; Colonial Records Project of, 16; commemorates 75th anniversary, 57; county histories by, 15; creation of, 4; document restoration by, 7-8; duties of, 4, 99; educational activities of, 5, 6; first secretary and staff of, 4; highway historical marker program of, 8-9, 19, 23, 49; historic preservation program of, 6, 24-25, 30; historic sites program of, 13, 20; iconographic collection of, 26; legislation broadening powers of, 2; legislation changing name to State Department of Archives and History, 27; legislation creating, 1-2, 4; legislation creating Legislative Reference Department within, 11; legislation to preserve prehistoric remains through, 20; legislation to protect and preserve public records through, 17, 19; legislation requiring approval of to place statuary in State Capitol, 8; membership of (2002), pictured, 99; microfilming program of, 26; military records collected by, 11, 12, 28; offices of, 7, 24-25; organizational meeting of, 1; original membership of, 1; poster collection of, 11; proposed transfer of to Department of Public Instruction, 13; publication of biennial reports by, 2, 17; publication on Civil War by, 4; publication of compendium of literary and historical activities by, 2; publication of county histories by, 15; publication of documentaries by, 2, 5, 17; publication of Moravian records by, 12; publication of *North Carolina Historical Review* by, 12, 14-15, 17; records storage facilities of, 7, 24-25

North Carolina Historical Review: augmented by *Carolina Comments*, 41, 55; contributors to, 15; desktop publishing technology utilized by, 93; under direction of Albert Ray Newsome, 12-13; under direction of David Leroy Corbitt, 15; editorial board of, 14; editors of, 12-13, 15; established by North Carolina Historical Commission, 12, 14; history of, 14-15; increased subscription prices of, 42; named by R. D. W. Connor, 12; soaring production costs of, 65; subscription to, provided to members of North Carolina Literary and Historical Association, 5; survives the depression, 17

North Carolina History Quiz, 40

North Carolina: The History of a Southern State, 14

North Carolina Humanities Council, 85

North Carolina Library Association, 39

North Carolina Literary and Historical Association: awards given by, 5, 40; hosts reception for Historical Publications Section, 93; keynote speakers at annual meetings of, 4; organization of, 4; sponsorship of Culture Week by, 5, 23

North Carolina Literary Review, 5

North Carolina Maritime Museum, 88, 89, 90

North Carolina Museum of History: accession records of, 50, 53; becomes autonomous division, 92; becomes division, 32; care of collections by, 50; education and outreach concerning demonstration of crafts at, 51-52; education and outreach through the World Wide Web, 41, 83; education and outreach with "Month of Sundays"

programs, 69; education and outreach with Tar Heel Junior Historian Association, 40-41, 50; exhibit of *The Black Presence in North Carolina*, 69, 70 (pictured); exhibit about Carbine Williams, 68-69, 71 (pictured); exhibit of *Health and Healing Experiences in North Carolina*, 92; exhibit of *North Carolina Women Making History*, 91; exhibit of *Raleigh & Roanoke*, 79, 80 (pictured), 81; exhibit about Thomas Day, 69; living history demonstrations by, 79; mobile museum of, 37-38, 47, 50; name changed from Hall of History to, 50; new building for, 50, 79, 91 (pictured), 92; publications of, 50, 73; regional branches of, 62, 78, 79, 89, 90; slide loan program of, 38; support group established for, 68; training of docents by, 50-52; transfer of documents to State Archives by, 53; transfer of iconographic collection to State Archives by, 67; utilization of automation by, 41, 73, 83. *See also* Hall of History

North Carolina Newspaper Project, 39, 53, 93

North Carolina Newspapers before 1790, 23

North Carolina Newspapers on Microfilm, 39

North Carolina Schools and Academies, 1790-1840, 5

North Carolina Shipbuilding Co., 29

North Carolina Society for the Preservation of Antiquities, 5, 24-25, 30, 94

North Carolina Society of the Cincinnati, 51

North Carolina State Archives: acquisition of Black Mountain College records by, 53; acquisition of Carolina Charter by, 32-33, 51; biographical directory of legislators compiled by, 81; cemetery survey of, 81; census records collected by, 29-30; Core Collection created by, 67; court cases involving, 67-69; development of Internet presence by, 83; development of Manuscript and Archives Reference System (MARS) by, 72, 73, 83; disaster recovery assistance given by, 87; distinguished service award received from Society of American Archivists by, 53; educational activities of, 66-67, 74; establishment of processing lab, 53; exhibits of, 66-67; hours of operation for, 52, 67; iconographic collection of, 26, 67; legislation concerning, 38, 40, 52-53; local records program of, 52, 53, 66; mandated to receive records of defunct colleges, 53; marriage bond index created by, 67; microfilming agreement with Genealogical Society of Utah to film county records in, 26; microfilming of Core Collection by, 67; microfilming by Local Records Section, 66; microfilming of newspapers by, 40, 53, 93; microfilming in State Records Center, 65; military records collected by, 28, 92; participation in international digitization project by, 92; publications of, 52, 92; purchase of flatbed camera by, 33; records management begun in earnest by, 33; records management contributions recognized by Society of American Archivists, 53; records management function returned to Division of Archives and History, 66; records management function transferred to Department of Administration, 65; records management of local records, 18, 52-53; records management through microfilming, 38; records management pioneered by Christopher Crittenden, 23; records management through records disposition schedules, 40, 53, 65; records management in State Records Center, 65-66; records management by State Records Section, 52-53; records management supported by Council of State, 40; records management supported by Governor Sanford, 53; records storage facilities of, in Administration Building, 7, 24; records storage facilities of, in Archives and History/State Library Building, 44-45, 52, 85; records storage facilities of, in Blount Street Annex, 92-93; records storage facilities of, in Education Building, 24-25, 43; records storage facilities of, in Old Records Center, 38, 40; records storage facilities of, in Old State Farmer's Market, 87; records storage facilities of, at State Fairgrounds, 33; records storage facilities of, in State Records Center, 66; space problems of, addressed by lease of Blount Street Annex, 92; space problems of, in Administration Building, 24; space problems of, in Archives and History/State Library Building, 44-45; space problems of, because of lack of records center, 38; space problems of, in Education Building, 43; support group established for, 68; theft of records from, 67-69; utilization of automation by, 67, 72, 83, 92

North Carolina State Committee on Conservation of Cultural Resources, 27

North Carolina State University School of Design, 64, 95

North Carolina Transportation History Foundation, 61

North Carolina Transportation Museum: development of, 60-61; exhibits of, 60; special events of, 97

North Carolina Troops, 1861-1865: A Roster, 42, 47

North Carolina Vietnam Veterans Memorial Statue, 81; pictured, 82

Northeastern Historic Places Office, 62

Norton, Janet N.: pictured, 99

O

Oak Plain School, 46

O'Brien, Gail W., 99

Office of Archives and History, 57, 98, 100

Old Homes and Gardens of North Carolina, 24

Old Salem, 30, 59

Old Salem Historic District, 30

Old State Records Center, 38, 40

Olds, Frederick Augustus, 1, 9, 53; biographical sketch of, 10; criticism of, 10; pictured, 10

Olson, David J., 100

Oral history projects, 78

Oteen Center, 90; pictured, 62

Outer Banks Community Foundation, 87

Outer Banks History Center, 72, 77; pictured, 77

Owens, William A., Jr., 15

P

Page, Walter Hines, 14
Palmer, Alice Freeman, Memorial Institute, 74
Papers of Archibald D. Murphey, The, 5
Papers of Randolph Abbott Shotwell, The, 17
Papers of Thomas Ruffin, The, 5
Papers of William Alexander Graham, The, 73
Papers of Zebulon Baird Vance, The, 54
Parker, Freddie L.: pictured, 99
Parker, R. Hunt, Memorial Award, 5
Paschal, Herb: pictured, 27
Patton, James W., 65
Peele, William J., 1, 2, 4; pictured, 2
Penn, John, 19
Perry, William G., 31
Pettigrew State Park, 22, 96
Phillips, U. B., 4
Pierson, W. W., 16
Pilot Mountain State Park, 75
Pioneer Living Days, 45, 60; pictured, 46
Pirates of Colonial North Carolina, The, 42
Pleasant Retreat Academy, 6; pictured, 6
Poe, Clarence, 2
Poe House, 79
Poff, Jan-Michael: pictured, 93
Polk, James K., Birthplace, 48, 60
Polk Memorial, 60
Portrait collection, 27, 50
Poster collection, 11
Powell, William S.: pictured, 37, 99
Pratt, Joseph Hyde, 25; pictured, 24
Preservation North Carolina, 25, 94
Preservation of historic buildings: architectural surveys concerning, 54-55, 64, 93-94; legislation concerning, 30, 63, 64, 94-95; by North Carolina Historical Commission, 6; by private organizations, 24-25; projects concerning, 63; tax credits for, 63, 94-95
Price, William, Jr., 69, 82; pictured, 66
Princeville, 86
Public History in North Carolina, 1903-1978, 57
Public Instruction, Department of. *See* Department of Public Instruction
Public Record Office, 16, 22
Public Records Act (1935), 17, 19
Publications by historical agencies: Archaeology and Historic Preservation Section, 93-94; Archives and Records Section, 92; Carolina Charter Tercentenary Commission, 51, 73; under direction of Christopher Crittenden, 23; discontinued for lack of funding, 18, 29; Division of Archives and History, 57, 85; Historic Sites Section, 74; Historical Publications Section, 54, 55, 65, 73, 81, 93; North Carolina American Revolution Bicentennial Commission, 58; North Carolina Confederate Centennial Commission, 42, 47; North Carolina Historical Commission, 2, 4, 5, 12, 14-15, 17, 93; North Carolina Museum of History, 73; State Department of Archives and History, 31, 39, 41-42, 52; State Historic Preservation Office, 94; Tar Heel Junior Historian Association, 40-41, 50, 73; Works Progress Administration, 18, 21

Q

Queen Anne's Revenge, 88-89

R

Raleigh Host Lions Club, 82
Raleigh *News and Observer*, 26-27
Raleigh Register, 39
Records management program: of Department of Archives and History, 33, 38, 40, 52-53; formulated by North Carolina Historical Commission, 18; for local records, 52-53; microfilming as a component of, 26, 38, 40; pioneered by Christopher Crittenden, 23; returned to Division of Archives and History, 66; transferred to Department of Administration, 65
Records of the Moravians in North Carolina, 12
Records storage facilities: in Administration Building, 7, 24; construction of Archives and History/State Library Building, 43-45, 52; construction of Old Records Center, 38, 40; construction of State Records Center, 66; in Education Building, 24-25, 37, 43; environmental

problems in, 66, 85, 87, 92; of Hall of History, 7, 24-25; lease of Blount Street Annex, 92; at Old State Farmers' Market, 87; renovation of Old Records Center, 66; at State Fairgrounds, 33

S